chaos to control

chaos to control

a practical guide to getting things done

Ciara Conlon

ORPEN PRESS

Orpen Press
Lonsdale House
Avoca Ave
Blackrock
Co. Dublin
Ireland

e-mail: info@orpenpress.com
www.orpenpress.com

Paperback ISBN: 978-1-871305-44-9
ePub ISBN: 978-1-871305-61-6
Kindle ISBN: 978-1-871305-62-3

Printed in the UK by the MPG Books Group

To Jeanne, who taught me that we cannot control the trials that life sends us, but we always have the ability to choose how to react.

We miss you.

preface

Traditionally the word 'productivity' conjured up images of factory floors and boardroom meetings. In recent years its image has changed somewhat; with the advancements in technology and the influx of smart phones, productivity is becoming a fad and having the latest productivity app is a must. With all the emphasis on *doing*, people forget the real goal of becoming productive. It's not just about doing more stuff, but also about identifying what's important, while eliminating what's not important and having time left over to live a happy and balanced life.

From an organisational perspective, workers who have a healthy work–life balance suffer from less stress and tend to be more productive. Along with these more apparent benefits, it is also important to highlight that each and every one of us can have a direct impact on economic recovery by becoming more personally productive. It may sound simplistic, but a 10 per cent increase in the productivity of each worker in the country could directly impact our competitiveness as a nation and increase our GDP.

The most important lesson I want you to take away from this book is that productivity is not just for governments, boardrooms and technology geeks. Productivity is about how you live your life by leaving space and time for those things that really matter.

This book came about as a result of two conversations, one of which was with the man who introduced me to the power of productivity – Gerrit Cloete; the other was with Kate Bashford, an inspirational woman who reminded me that ten minutes a day can write a book. Thank you, Kate and Gerrit.

Thank you to my first readers and editors, Colette, Jamie and Kay, for taking the time and giving me the encouragement to make it happen. Thank you to my official editor at Orpen Press, Elizabeth, and to Ailbhe and Nuala for all your work in making my words available. And to Rachel McGuinness who has put great time and effort into making me an author.

Thank you to all my friends who repeatedly tell me I'm great, especially Córa, Grainne and Karina; to my four sisters who would like to believe they are my friends too, but they are so much more than that! Thanks to my South African sisters and to Almero and Adela who showed me that real love and acceptance don't only come with blood. Thank you, Kay and Val, my pillars in life, for always being there to listen, advise and give love.

And thanks to the four men in my house, Ockie, Jordan, Kai and Troy, who make me laugh and cry (all before breakfast). I love you to infinity plus a googol. Thank you for giving me the time, the love and the occasional box of smiles to help me fulfil my dreams.

Ek is baie lief vir julle.

contents

introduction

Modern life has changed our priorities drastically over the last century. Life has changed from being survival of the fittest to being survival of the most technologically savvy. We crave more money, more gadgets, more responsibility, more stimulation, more distraction. Many of us have forgotten what really brings us joy. Some haven't forgotten, but think that they must delay their happiness until some day in the future – the day when all the technology and "busyness" has paid off and they have reached their earthly nirvana: a place called financial success. But, by that stage, they may be too old, too detached or too burnt out to relax and enjoy their family, friends and hobbies.

What we need to come to terms with is that there is only one thing certain in this world – the *current moment*. The past is gone and the future is not guaranteed. No matter how much planning you do, the outcome is not definite. Delaying gratification can be necessary sometimes, but if we spend our days blindly running from one task to the next we may be missing out on the happiness and success we can achieve in the current moment. A great portion of individuals are unhappy, dissatisfied or stressed, but it doesn't have to be this way.

I'm not suggesting for one minute that you should throw caution to the wind and stop planning for the future, that you can now spend all your savings and cancel the health insurance. I am saying that there should be a balance. We must plan for the future – otherwise it will not be very comfortable or secure – but we need to plan and work in such a way that allows us to enjoy our lives as much as possible. We should be aiming to reduce our stress, and to work in an efficient and productive manner so that our work is done well and in the minimum time possible.

Now is the time to change the way we think about work. Being busier does not define self-worth; it probably means you don't work as effectively as you should. Filling the hours of a working day does not necessarily mean you got lots of work done; it just means you spend eight hours doing something. Now is the time to take back the control and start to work in a more systematic and methodical way in order to allow yourself enough time to appreciate the passing moments of your life. Working productively and organising your life in an efficient manner enables you to have a healthy and happy work–life balance. Whether you work for yourself and or work for an organisation, productivity can help to reduce stress and give you more sense of control over your life. The benefits of productivity are not just related to saving time; productivity and organisation induce a sense of calm control and can contribute to greater achievement and success.

What you can expect from this book

This book consists of seven sections. Each section will introduce you to a concept that will assist you in living to your full potential by helping you to become more focused, organised and positive. You will be encouraged to adopt new habits, each habit taking you closer to your goals and your success.

Section 1 – Vision: This section includes lots of tips and reasons why having a clearly defined vision and setting goals contribute to a much higher possibility of accomplishing all that you want to achieve. Creating a vision and setting goals effectively are the cornerstones of all things productive. Without a vision and goals how do you know if the work you are doing is what you should be doing? Would your time be better spent on a different task? Knowing what you want from your life keeps you on track; it inspires you to continue with a particular task, as you know this task is helping you reach your goals. Having a vision motivates you; it gives you a reason to get out of bed in the morning and it inspires you to keep moving forwards towards your greater success.

Section 2 – Awareness: Knowing how you currently work and what you spend your time on can be invaluable in order to move forwards and make informed and knowledgeable decisions. The importance of awareness is often ignored, but many agree that awareness of your present status will bring you a great deal further along the road to success. If you wish to work more productively, the first thing you should know is how you are currently spending your time: are you a time waster or a busy fool? Increasing awareness is essential to being able to rectify bad habits, adjust and stay in control of your life.

Section 3 – Systems: Productivity systems can help you to work proficiently and effectively. Adopting an effective system will enable you to remain in control and focused at all times. From "Getting Things Done" – productivity guru David Allen's infamous workflow management system – to minimalism, your system can shape and define your world and your world of work. Most workers can do their jobs, but few can organise themselves efficiently and create a flow of work that prevents them from wasting time or getting distracted by their friends at the water cooler!

Section 4 – Technology: Section four considers the undeniable force in our lives that is technology. Technology assisted the growth and development of many industries over the last century. It has been of enormous benefit to productivity and efficiency. On the other hand, it can be a productivity killer, distracting us from our goals and scheduled tasks. This section suggests many ways to use technology to your advantage and gain from the multitude of systems and programs that can make your life easier.

Section 5 – Leadership and Productivity: Effective leadership by means of enhanced productivity is the subject matter of this section. The obvious benefits of enhanced productivity are even more apparent when the productive individual is a leader. Leaders will lead more successfully if they are productive themselves. A good team will learn from their mentor, and if the mentor sets good examples the team will follow.

Section 6 – Positivity: The power of positivity is sometimes undervalued. Research shows that optimists are healthier, wealthier and more successful in life. Research shows that happy people are more productive in the workplace. By engaging with positive psychology we can not only improve our own lives but also the lives of those around us. With positivity come positive habits. Good habits will assist us on our journey to greater happiness and success.

Section 7 – Maintaining the Flow: The purpose of the final section in this book is to support you on your journey. It contains much advice about how to stay focused, avoid procrastination, maintain those positive habits and preserve all that you have learnt.

section 1 – vision

1

the vision

look beyond what the eye can see

> "Our plans miscarry because they have
> no aim. When a man does not know what
> harbour he is making for, no wind is the
> right wind."
>
> – Seneca

Golfer Tiger Woods spends countless hours every day hitting balls. Tennis greats like André Agassi and Pete Sampras spent much of their childhood on the tennis courts. When most of us may have given up, leaders in their field persist, and what allows them to persist is a fierce focus that they don't allow to falter. This focus is based on their vision. They are 100 per cent clear about what they want to accomplish in life and having this clarity assists in their endurance and focus.

Steven Covey expressed it well in his book *The 7 Habits of Highly Effective People*: "Begin with the end in mind." Being crystal clear about your higher goals and final outcomes will most definitely help you to achieve them sooner. Having a vision for the future, which you are passionate about, helps you to connect with your daily tasks on a higher level. If you know that all you do is for a greater purpose, i.e. to help you to reach your personal paradise more quickly, this will become the motivation that will inspire you should you need an incentive to carry out your daily tasks in an efficient and effective manner.

By connecting with your personal vision, you have taken the first step to creating your own future – the future that only you can visualise, custom made for you. Creating a vision for the future is a step that should not be ignored. Designing an image for the future is a primary element in becoming a highly productive individual. Knowing where you are headed assists greatly in knowing if the route you are on and the targets you are aiming for are the correct ones, and ultimately if the tasks you busy yourself with daily are the ones that will get you closer to your success.

In 1963 one man had a vision which was to change history:

> I have a dream that my four little children will one day live in a nation where they will not be judged by the color of their skin but by the content of their character. I have that dream today.

Martin Luther King's famous speech was delivered on 28 August 1963 to civil rights supporters on the steps of the Lincoln Memorial in Washington. It is credited with bringing about the 1964 Civil Rights Act. The mental picture that he had created for the future of America was shared that day with 250,000 people, and he made this dream a reality. His dream changed the lives of millions of people.

Creating a vision

Abraham Maslow was an American psychologist who is most widely known for his theory of personality known as the "hierarchy of needs", which formed part of his 1943 paper *A Theory of Human Motivation*.

He suggested that people have needs that have to be satisfied, and that it is possible to arrange those needs in a hierarchical list. This hierarchy means that the lower-level needs must be satisfied before the higher levels can become motivational factors for the individual.

Maslow stated that our physiological needs must be satisfied first – food and drink are the first motivators of man – but once these are satisfied, we then look for shelter and security. As our more basic needs are satisfied, we rise up the hierarchy to satisfy our social needs and self-esteem needs before reaching the stage of self-actualisation.

We can look at creating our vision in the form of a hierarchy also; it may not be possible to have a clear picture of your vision until some lower-level work has been completed.

Daily tasks and responsibilities

These include the countless tasks that we must do daily – paperwork, washing, ironing, shopping, computer work, phone calls, etc.

Projects

These include any work that needs doing, holidays to be planned, rooms to be redecorated, fundraisers to be organised and work projects to be completed. Projects can also include the "Oh, I must do something about that" things, such as the wedding album that you still haven't put together after seven years of marriage.

Goals and objectives

You must set long- or short-term goals to achieve certain objectives in your life – financial goals, health goals, work goals. You should also understand the reasons why you want to achieve them.

Vision

Your vision is your view of what long-term success looks like and what your plan is for your future. It is a good idea to have a positive vision of the future which will inspire you to work towards it. If you don't have a clear plan, you can lack the motivation to work hard and set the goals necessary to achieve your long-term vision. Hard work isn't so hard if you know there is a reward at the end.

Purpose

Being in alignment with your higher purpose can give you clarity and personal freedom to pursue your vision and goals. Without this, you may experience disorder and confusion in your mind, rather than calm and ease with yourself.

It is very important to be clear about your vision and goals in order to work productively. However, if your daily tasks are overwhelming you and you can't seem to clear the clutter, it can be difficult to relax and truly visualise what it is you want out of life. If you are living your life on a treadmill and working sixty hours a week to cover your costs, spending time thinking about your life purpose can seem like a joke.

For this reason, a two-pronged approach makes more sense. In order to achieve the maximum effect and attain true success we must be clear about our vision and purpose in life. As we clear the disorder and confusion in our environment and in our heads, our vision and purpose will become more and more apparent. Later chapters explore the ways in which we can control the disorder and clutter in our lives. The best presentations, speeches and holidays were all achieved by having an initial idea and then focusing on the preparation and planning. From this moment forward everything you do should tie in with the image you have of your perfect life. In this way, every action you take and every goal you set are taking you closer to your ideal world and life. Every deed, every act should have a purpose. Start by working on your vision, but as you become more organised and your life less stressed and cluttered, you may find that your vision has changed and that you may need to adjust it. Human beings are dynamic and your world and view of your world will be ever-changing. But once you start to focus on your vision, you will be amazed at how quickly your future will materialise.

Working on your personal vision

There are many ways to work on developing your vision of your ideal life. One of the best ways to visualise the ideal is to imagine yourself at the end of your life, or even at your own funeral, and ask yourself how you would like to be remembered. At this stage you don't need to worry about the how, you just want to create a picture that truly excites and inspires you.

What kind of person were you? Write down how you would like your family and friends to speak about you.
Examples:
He was a kind and caring father who always had time for his children.
She was a supportive and loving mother who lived her life thinking of others.
He was a successful businessman who always put his clients first.

How would you like to be remembered in business? What legacy would you be happy to leave behind?

Are you working towards this vision now?

Another way is to picture your ideal future.

What would you do if there were no restrictions and no boundaries?

Answer the following questions:

What would you do if you knew you couldn't fail?

How would you spend your days if you won €4 billion in the Lotto?

These questions allow you to dream big. They make sure you are not restricting your vision by the boundaries and limitations that we place on our lives.

Consider Michelangelo's words before creating your vision:

> "The greater danger for most of us lies
> not in setting our aim too high and falling
> short; but in setting our aim too low, and
> achieving our mark."

Visualising and setting your sights on the prize gives you an idea of how you will feel when you achieve your vision. This process of daydreaming and letting your senses feel, see and taste the goal will make you feel inspired and motivated. If you don't feel excited about your future vision then maybe it's time to think about a different one!

Writing it down is paramount to your success. Revisiting what you've written daily will help you to remember what it is you want, and keep it in the realm of your subconscious.

Another way to work on your personal vision is to create a vision board or a picture book, which is a visual representation of what you want to achieve. The idea is to keep a visual display of your ideal life in your view so that your subconscious mind will absorb the images and help you to work towards these goals. Your brain responds well to picture images so the more you look at these images, the more they become part of your brain's reality. You can also create a vision map by using some mind-mapping software or by simply drawing your own vision map. By doing so, you are allowing your mind to be creative and relax into the thoughts, plans and dreams for the future. You may think that grown-up men and women don't play around with pictures, scissors and glue, but if you open your mind to doing something different and creative you might be surprised at what can materialise.

Creating a company vision

As with your personal vision, a company vision must represent the uniqueness of your organisation, what it stands for and what it wants to achieve. A lot of companies will already have a vision statement, the purpose of which is to create a mental picture that can serve to energise and inspire you and your company. A powerful vision should stretch expectations. It should push the boundaries of what you deem possible.

Take a look at Microsoft's vision:

> "A personal computer in every home,
> running Microsoft software."

Gate's vision for Microsoft is simple and powerful and can be visualised by all levels of the organisation. When this vision was created, it was probably considered a very tall order, and some might say that aiming so high can set an organisation up for failure. Microsoft has not achieved its vision of having a PC in every home, but it has far exceeded many people's expectations of what would have been deemed possible. Therefore we would never say they have failed but that there is still room for improvement.

Ray Kroc's vision for McDonald's was that people could find fast, tasty food wherever they travelled. One of the goals of McDonald's was that the food in all of its stores – all over the world – would taste exactly the same. He wanted their customers to have a clean, pleasant place to eat in. This is clear in the McDonald's vision statement:

> "To be the world's best quick service restaurant experience. McDonald's accomplishes this by providing each customer with outstanding quality, service, cleanliness and value."

In 1998 Larry Page and Sergey Brin set out to change the world of the internet. They wanted to organise every bit of information on the web for free. They had a vision for Google which not only seemed farfetched but was probably considered impossible for two young students to achieve. Not only have Brin and Page achieved what they set out to do, but they did so within the boundaries of their guiding mantra of "Do no evil."

Their corporate vision was:

> "To organise the world's information and make it universally accessible and useful."

What is impressive about these vision statements, apart from the fact that they are very ambitious, is that so many employees at all levels in all of these organisations would be aware of and support the company's vision. Successful companies have a shared vision that everyone in the organisation is willing to work towards. Giving people a purpose towards which to work can greatly increase motivation and productivity.

Your vision must be in alignment with your values and principles

Most of us have some sort of a vision for the future, but very often this vision is one that has been created for us by our boss or our partner, or perhaps we created it ourselves through a logical thought process of what should come next.

Many organisations promote the team member with the most experience to the position of manager. As we all know too well, management involves a lot more than experience. But because management is a prestigious position and one that usually comes with more money and more benefits, most people would not refuse the opportunity. But is management right for everybody? Does it fit in with everybody's values and principles? The answer, of course, is no. It is important not to accept what people want for you or believe you are capable of. You must decide those things for yourself; whatever your vision or plans for the future are, they must be in alignment with your values.

So if your vision is to own a cigarette company and you detest smoking, this is probably going to cause some internal conflict. Or if you want to buy shares in an oil company but you work for Greenpeace, you may find at some level you will sabotage your achievement of this goal. So make sure what you are hoping to achieve in the future in is in harmony with your true values.

Write down your vision statement, either your personal vision or that of your company. Now take a look at the questions below:

What are you trying to achieve?

Does your vision respect your beliefs and your values?

Does your vision embody the spirit of your company?

2

goal setting

the setting in stone

"First say to yourself what you would be;
and then do what you have to do."

– Epictetus

Goal setting

After creating your long-term vision or ideal picture of your life, goals can assist you in breaking these down into achievable objectives.

Setting goals is a habit all highly successful and effective people share. By setting goals and having a personal or professional plan of what you want to achieve, you are much more likely to keep on track and stay inspired. Always know what your motivations are. If you know your reasons and your motivations for doing a certain task, you will be more encouraged to complete it.

Goals, when correctly set, can be extremely motivating. As you create and achieve goals, you will find it a rewarding process, and your confidence will grow as you achieve more and more goals. The process also helps you to organise your time and resources in an effective manner, helping you to achieve and accomplish all that you desire.

Goals are the actions you will take to make these changes in your life happen. Goals make up the blueprint or the strategy that will take you to your ideal life. As with your vision, make sure that your goals are what you yourself want to achieve and not what someone else expects from you.

Criteria for setting goals

There are many schools of thought as to what is important when it comes to goal setting. There are some important criteria to consider when setting your goals, which are likely to make your goals more accessible and attainable.

When writing down your goals, state exactly what it is you wish to achieve. Someone else should be able to read your goals and understand exactly what it is you are aiming for.

Is your goal specific? In 1990, Locke and Latham, two American psychologists, published a piece of work in which they stated that goal-directed effort was a function of four goal attributes: difficulty, specificity, acceptance and commitment.[1] Goal specificity refers to the degree of clarity around the goal: increasing sales is not specific, but increasing sales by 10 per cent by the end of the year is. According to a study by Latham and Yukl, specificity has been shown to be consistently related to performance.[2]

How will you know when you have achieved your goal? A goal should also be measureable in some form. Breaking

---

[1] Edwin A. Locke and Gary P. Latham, *A Theory of Goal Setting and Task Performance*, New Jersey: N.J. Prentice Hall Inc, 1990.
[2] Gary P. Latham and Gary A. Yukl, "A Review of Research on the Application of Goal Setting in Organizations", *Journal of Applied Psychology*, vol. 60, 1975, pp. 187–91.

it into parts makes it easier to measure and see results. It is a way to gauge what has been accomplished to date. Don't just write, "I want to lose weight." State how much weight you want to lose and by what date.

Is your goal achievable? If you set yourself a goal that is not physically possible to achieve, you are only setting yourself up for failure and disappointment. Some might say anything is achievable if you put your mind to it, but if you hope to run the Boston Marathon in May and in February of the same year you break your leg, you must admit to yourself that this goal is not achievable.

But remember, as Locke and Latham point out, easy-to-achieve goals are not motivational. If a goal lacks challenge there is no motivation to achieve it, but, on the flipside, if a goal is too difficult and too challenging, we may not step outside our comfort zone to try and achieve it.

Should your goal be realistic? It is good to set big goals, but if they are unrealistic and physically not possible for you to achieve, this can have a negative impact. Set interim, more realistic goals that can be achieved and that make the ultimate goal more feasible. It is important to be realistic when setting goals, but being too realistic is something we have to be careful of. One of the problems with goal setting is that people set goals inside the boundaries of their limited imagination; when they look at setting realistic goals, they become too realistic and they start to try and figure out the route to achieving that goal. If the route to achievement is visible then they decide it is a realistic goal, but if they cannot visualise how they will achieve this goal they deem it to be unrealistic. It is important not to limit your potential according to the limits of your own imagination. Imagine a reality where everyone harnessed their full potential. Wouldn't the world be a very different place? Very often, our goals will materialise bit by bit and things will change gradually through our own hard work and through luck and coincidence. If you look back at your life and contemplate some of the events that have happened you will see that at times some of the results were caused by things that you would never have deemed possible. Allow yourself some goals that to others may appear unrealistic, but inside you know you can achieve someday, somehow.

Can you visualise the achievement of the goal? Goals that you can visualise, taste or smell are more likely to materialise. If you want a new car, visualise yourself inside the car. What does the dashboard look like? What can you see all around you? Imagine how it would make you feel to drive your new car – the rush of excitement and adrenaline as you put your foot on the accelerator. Imagine the smell of the leather seats, the new-car smell.

If goal setting is a new activity for you, it is a good idea to set a range of goals in different areas of your life and with different levels of achievability. Also, never forget to ask yourself the reason why you want to achieve this goal. What will it mean to you if you achieve or accomplish this goal? Knowing the purpose of achieving the goal aids motivation and completion and can help to inspire and maintain enthusiasm if you have lost the incentive to continue.

Goal-setting tools

The reminder

We all have goals: some that we set over and over again, some that we achieve, some that we don't. A goal is something that we have set because it is something we would like to have or something we would like to achieve. We need encouragement and motivation to achieve some goals. For others we need good luck or simply hard work. But for all goals it is a good idea to remind ourselves why we want to achieve them in the first place.

So you want to lose weight: *Why?* Because you want to be slim and healthy.
The why can be a motivator.

You want to earn enough money: *Why?* So you can give your family the life they deserve.
The why can give it purpose.

You want to run a marathon: *Why?* Because you want to challenge yourself and your boundaries.
The why can be your inspiration.

After fifteen hours of labour with my first child, my energy was depleting and the risk of the birth not turning out to be a natural one was becoming more likely. I wanted a natural birth, but I didn't have much more to give. Then one of the midwives, who I will always remember with fondness, asked me where my bag was. At the time I remember feeling irritated as I couldn't figure out why she wanted to poke around in my bag, when, as far as I was concerned, her focus should have been on helping me deliver the baby! She then came over to me with the smallest and most precious piece of clothing ever. She held up one of the baby suits I had in my bag and asked if I was happy with the one she had chosen to be the baby's first outfit. She said she would place it on the radiator so it would be nice and warm for the baby when he was born. A very clever trick! After so many hours of pain and self-absorbed misery, I had forgotten why I was in this position. I had forgotten that this labour was not in vain, that it had purpose. Her reminder gave me the last boost of energy necessary to push my beautiful boy out. He was born fifteen minutes after I saw his little baby suit! Sometimes all we need is a little reminder of why we want to achieve the goal in the first place to give us the inspiration to keep going.

Beliefs and attitude

Remember the words of Henry Ford – "Whether you think you can or whether you think you can't, you're right." You must believe in your goals and in your power to achieve them. Don't allow negative self-talk or negative "other people's talk" to stand in the way of your dreams. There is a lot of negativity out there and there are a lot of well-meaning people who will try to restrict your goals with their limited thinking.

A large percentage of our beliefs are instilled in us when we are children. We are conditioned by the people who surround us as we grow. Our parents, our teachers, our siblings and all those around us have an influence on how we perceive ourselves, our capabilities and talents. It is surprising the number of adults who live their lives based on the beliefs that their parents or teachers have instilled in them. Many adults will tell you their teachers told them they would amount to nothing, or their parents advised them that they shouldn't aim too high in case they would be disappointed. There are countless beliefs that surface in adulthood, that, when scrutinised, can reveal themselves as untrue, but which may have been holding a person back for most of their adult life.

Belief systems can dominate our thinking. Think back to not too long ago when the dominant thought paradigm was that the earth was at the centre of the universe. Stepping outside this paradigm was to risk ridicule. We all hold many beliefs about the world and about ourselves. Sometimes the beliefs we have about ourselves can be as misguided as the accepted view of the universe prior to the sixteenth century.

Challenging your current beliefs can be an important step in the goal-setting process:

Take a look at your own beliefs. Were your dreams encouraged or frowned upon as a child?

Do you have limiting beliefs which prevent you from fulfilling your dreams? Do you ever say the words, "I could never do that"?

If you are guilty of setting yourself limitations, are there genuine reasons for this or are they misguided paradigms that you have created?

A winning attitude

The film *La vita è bella* (*Life Is Beautiful*) tells the story of a Jewish Italian who is taken prisoner by the Nazis and sent to a concentration camp with his four-year-old son. In order to keep his boy in good spirits and from missing his mother, he explains to him that it is all a game. If the boy stays quiet and out of sight he will earn points, but if he cries for his mother he will lose points. His positive attitude keeps the boy in good spirits and ultimately saves the boy's life. Thankfully, in the large part, not being able to achieve our goals doesn't have such extreme consequences, but this example shows how our attitude to life, our trials and our successes is what decides our quality of life. Having a good attitude means taking responsibility for our actions and not playing the victim. Victims blame external circumstances for their failings and their bad luck.

As a life coach I often hear people say, "I don't have time to exercise" or "I'm too tired when I get home from work" or "I have too many responsibilities", and so on. People like to think that when the next project in work finishes they will have more time, or when the evenings become brighter they won't feel so tired. They are always pushing their lives into the future and avoiding the now. These are excuses, and excuses like these are made by victims. I have definitely been a victim in the past, and I continue to be at times in the present, but I remind myself and I try to ask myself regularly, "Am I playing victim? Or is there a genuine reason for not moving towards my goals?"

Nelson Mandela could have played the victim. He spent twenty-eight years imprisoned, and on a couple of occasions was offered freedom in exchange for giving up his fight. He consistently refused to compromise his political position in order to obtain his freedom. When Mandela was finally released from prison in 1990, his attitude was noted and observed by the world. Mandela didn't show resentment or bitterness towards the people who put him there; he even included some of the people who had kept him in prison in his first cabinet as leader. Mandela knew that if he bore hatred and resentment there would never be a united South Africa. For peace and integration to ensue, his attitude had to be one of peace and acceptance. What had happened was in the past and the future of reconciliation could only be achieved with a new attitude.

Don't waste time playing the blame game; put your past mistakes and excuses behind you and take control of your future. Like a beautiful friend once told me, we cannot control the trials that life sends us but we always have the ability to choose how we react.

Writing down your goals

Writing down your goals is a powerful part of the goal-setting process. Putting it down on paper commits you to doing something about the goal. When you begin to write down the goal, you formulate a picture of what you want to achieve in your subconscious, and as you write you will find you become clearer about your objectives. When the goal is written down, you can revisit it regularly to check your progress. But there is another more powerful reason for writing down your goals.

The part of the human brain concerned with arousal and activity is called the Reticular Activating System or RAS. The RAS makes sure that the brain stays alert and awake when necessary. One of the responsibilities of the RAS is to control sensory input to the brain. When the brain perceives that there is too much stimulus, the RAS will not allow this extra stimulus into the brain, thus acting like a filter. This so-called filter helps us survive in a world with high levels of activity and stimulus.

The brain can receive and respond to sensory information without this data entering into consciousness. However, if this stimulus is repeated (e.g. a baby's cry), it will normally result in conscious awareness. This is because the RAS has been activated.

Have you ever noticed that once you are conscious of something, you begin to notice it everywhere? For example, you buy a new car and when you pull out of the showroom you see the same car in the same colour everywhere you look. Or if your wife is pregnant, all of a sudden you see babies, prams and pregnant women all around. It's not that these cars weren't on the road a day earlier, nor is it the fact that extra babies were born to accompany you and your partner through the next stages of your life. It is simply that the RAS has subconsciously noted the relevant surroundings and has passed this information to your conscious mind. You have allowed your filter to include this new information that previously wasn't any concern of yours. Once certain information becomes relevant to you, the RAS will respond to any activity or stimulus that concerns you.

Can you see how this affects your ability to get what you want and your ability to achieve your goals? You get what you focus on; you receive what you give attention to. By writing down your goals or by creating a vision board for your goals, you are allowing these items into your life and into your filtering system. If you did not pay attention to your vision or your goals, your subconscious mind would not be concerned with the events that occur in relation to these goals. When you write down your goals and pay attention to them, you will see boundless opportunities and so-called coincidences come your way.

Another aspect to be aware of is that your brain does not know the difference between a positive and negative statement. If you are told not to think about a big hairy ape with a large yellow banana, what image do you create in your head whilst not trying to think about it? So, if you are constantly saying "I don't want to have debt," your brain is thinking "debt, debt, debt". The conscious mind sends this to the unconscious mind and this becomes your focus. This is why, when setting goals, you must think in the positive rather than in the negative. Instead of saying "I don't want to be in debt anymore", try "I wish to have an abundance of money to pay for all my needs and requirements in life." Because the subconscious mind has such an influence on our lives, it means that we can practise a very powerful trick to help us to manifest our goals more quickly and with less difficulty.

The power of visualisation

There are many books written on the power of visualisation, so much so that visualisation techniques have become very much a part of sports and business training and practice. Visualisation is the simple process of creating a picture in your mind's eye of your ideal outcome.

The golfer Jack Nicklaus, in his book *Golf My Way*, writes that he never hits a shot, even in practice, without having a sharp picture of it in his mind first. Leading entrepreneurs and peak performers will visualise and play out in their minds the scenarios they want to occur in their lives. Part of most sportspeople's preparation for a match or an event is to imagine the final outcome. They have an image of the hole in one or the ace serve, so that their body believes it has done that shot or that serve countless times before. The subconscious mind doesn't know the difference between the real and the imagined experience.

It is widely believed that imagery and visualisation can be very effective in healing. There is no hard evidence to prove that it works, but there are countless individual cases that the body can be positively affected by just visualising the healing process. Think about cutting into a fat juicy yellow lemon. As you cut it, the juice squirts out and some of it runs down the side of your hand, you can smell it and before you put it to your mouth you have started to salivate. This proves the power of the mind. The mind can induce physical reactions in the body.

Paul McKenna, the world-leading hypnotist and author, suggests that we should create our visualisations on a large silver screen, allowing us to make the images crisp and clear and as large as we like. He recommends that we increase in size the positive images that we want to imprint in the brain, but that we should make the images we want to forget, such as bad memories, really small, out of focus and distant, making them less reachable.

To begin visualisation, it is best to be in a calm and relaxed state. Maybe start with some breathing exercises. Then relax, close your eyes and bring to mind the picture you wish to create. Try to use all your senses, while visualising and imagining what you can see, what you can hear, and what you can taste, smell and feel. The senses will assist in making the image more powerful and more realistic to the subconscious. Some recommend doing this visualisation exercise every morning and every evening to assist you in reaching your goals.

The influence of affirmations

"I am the greatest."

– Mohammed Ali

One of the most powerful and well-known affirmations ever used, Mohammed Ali admitted that he started to use this catchphrase long before he ever believed it. He reckoned that if he used it often enough he would eventually convince everyone and himself that it was true!

Affirmations – simple positive statements – help to programme the brain to be more positive. I am calm; I am the greatest; I am busy building the life of my dreams – whatever the positive statement is, the more that it is repeated the more your brain will come to believe it.

There is a constant narrative going on daily in our brains. Every thought that we have, whether deliberate or unconscious, is a type of affirmation. Stop and take a look at the thoughts inside your head – are they positive or negative? Start to notice how you speak to yourself during the day. Become aware of the negative thoughts and pinch yourself each time you have one. Each time you put yourself down; each time you say something bad or disrespectful to somebody; each time you believe yourself incapable of achieving something, pinch yourself!

An affirmation should consist of the following key components:

- It should be positive.
- It should be in the present tense.
- It should exude emotion and enthusiasm.
- It should be graphically visual.

If you can visualise using your affirmations daily, your positive messages will be committed to your subconscious mind.

Then you can relax in the knowledge that you are no longer working alone.

The self-fulfilling prophecy

Can the mind transform predictions of the future into reality? Scientists believe that it can. They believe that people have a strong tendency to perform in a way that is expected of them. We have all learned that expectations of a child's performance can have a very strong influence on how a child ultimately does in school. In the workplace, most workers will perform only as far as what is expected of them. Few will exceed expectations. Stereotypes have constricted, and can constrict, how people behave and conform according to what is expected.

Dr Sara Bengtsson,[3] a cognitive neuroscientist, carried out studies to see if students' performance on a cognitive task could be influenced by priming these students with the words "clever" or "stupid". She found that simply presenting the student with the word would affect their performance of the task, even though these words were irrelevant to the person's true ability. But this irrelevant information unconsciously affected the students' expectations of themselves and thus changed their performance. These studies were being carried out while the students' brains were being scanned for activity in certain areas of the brain. What the study showed was that the students' brains responded differently when they learned they had made a mistake, depending on whether they had been previously primed with the word clever or with the word stupid. When they were given the word clever and then made an error, enhanced activity was observed in the medial prefrontal cortex of the brain. This increased activity was not observed after people gave a correct answer or

---

[3] See Tali Sharot, *The Optimism Bias: A Tour of the Irrationally Positive Brain*, UK: Pantheon Books, 2011.

when they had previously been given the word stupid. The theory is that the activity in the medial prefrontal cortex of the brain occurs when a person's expectations do not agree with the outcome. In the brains of those who expected to do well (the students with the word clever), the brain reacted to this mismatch. However, the participants in the study who expected to do badly had no increased activity in this area of the brain, because the brain got what it expected.

When the brain doesn't get what it expects, it tries to figure out what went wrong. The importance of this is that it facilitates learning. If our brain takes notice of something going wrong, usually this is when we learn from our error and try again. Learning from our errors leads to better performance.

In general, the frontal lobes of the brain mediate planning and action to achieve the goals we have identified for ourselves. Progress towards our goals is monitored by matching what we do with what we expect. If we don't achieve what we expect, we are more likely to assess the reasons and identify new actions.

So if we don't set goals and have positive expectations about our future, we will continue our normal lives and routines and should not be surprised that nothing improves or changes in our lives.

Setting goals encourages the realisation of a self-fulfilling prophecy. The fact that we write the goal down and commit to it gives us a much higher probability of achieving positive outcomes than someone who sets no goals.

What about failure?

Many people are tempted to say, "It's better not to wish for too much because you may be disappointed." Tali Sharot refers to this in her book *The Optimism Bias*. According to Sharot, holding low expectations to protect us from disappointment is known as defensive pessimism, but having low expectations doesn't reduce the pain of failure. She says that, not only do negative expectations lead to worse results, but they fail to protect us from negative emotions when we don't achieve our desired outcomes. Studies show that students who expect to do badly in exams and then get what they expected are no less disappointed than students who expected to do well and didn't.

You may not always achieve what you try for but persistence allows you to succeed. A student of mine once said, "Should we not say that failure is a prerequisite to success?" He suggested that we need to fail to grow and learn because it's only when we fail and make mistakes that we advance and develop. I don't think it is always necessary to fail, because sometimes prior preparation can get you what you are striving for, but it can be expected that we will all fail or make a mistake at something, sometime. Whether this mistake is in business or in our personal life, we will grow and learn and move on. But remember that, when we do fail, there is a lesson to be learned and potential for growth not to be overlooked.

Let your motto be: Learn, change, evolve.

Action plans and goal progress

The goal plan, the one-, two- or three-year plan, sets out a time frame for when you would like to have achieved certain goals. These goal plans help you to visualise the future. We also need to set short-term goals or milestones so we can check progress regularly. If you decide you want to run a marathon in twelve months' time, what will you need to have achieved by three months, by six months, etc. Breaking down your goals into smaller chunks makes them more achievable and attainable. You can also set yourself weekly tasks, which, when accomplished, will provide motivation and inspiration for you to continue. Each mini-goal achieved should be taking you closer and closer to your ultimate goals.

A weekly action plan should consist of all the tasks that need to be completed for the week, plus the weekly targets which you have set for yourself. At the beginning of the week, you should ask yourself, "What one thing can I do this week to take me closer to achieving my goals?"

Checking progress also allows you to realign your goals if things aren't going to plan. If you find you are not achieving the goals you have set yourself, you will need to ask yourself why. Is the goal realistic? Have you set yourself a challenge that is not physically possible to achieve? You must also look at the other commitments in your life and see if these are going to be affected if you pursue your goal. If you find real obstacles in your path, you may have to create some action plans to try and remove them.

And if you still believe that success is all down to luck, just remember one thing: The harder you work, the luckier you will get!

Productivity tips from Section 1 – Vision

1. Be clear about your vision.
2. Write a vision statement and/or create a vision board or map.
3. Make sure the goal is what you want, and not what society or others think should be your next step.
4. Believe you can achieve it.
5. Don't allow negative thoughts or so called "realism" prevent you from achieving your dreams.
6. Write down your goals.
7. Practise visualisation and affirmations.
8. Check progress regularly and eliminate any obstacles.

section 2 – awareness

3

awareness

awareness precedes control

"He who knows others is wise. He who knows himself is enlightened."

– Lao Tzu

It's a natural tendency of human beings to look outside and find a reason to explain their current circumstances rather than looking inside themselves to see how they personally are contributing to the present situation. A good leader cannot lead others if he doesn't know how to lead himself. An employer will find it difficult to have an efficient and productive workplace if he himself is disorganised and unproductive. A parent cannot expect order and discipline from a child if he himself has none.

Robin Sharma says, "Awareness precedes mastery." Before you can improve on your current circumstances, you must be crystal clear what those circumstances are. This is the first step in any change process. What is your starting point? All businesses begin with a SWOT analysis to establish its strengths, weaknesses, opportunities and threats.

Therefore, before we look at what we can do to become more efficient and productive, let us look at where we presently stand and what we are currently focusing our attention on. Are we stressed because we have too much work to do? Or are we busy and stressed because we are not focusing on the right work at the right time? All too often, people get stressed or overwhelmed by work simply because they are not doing the work that needs to be done or because they are spending too much time on unnecessary tasks.

Knowing your goals and objectives is one thing, but are you spending your typical day moving yourself closer towards these goals or are you allowing distractions and non-essential work to delay their acquisition?

Pareto productivity

Are you familiar with the Pareto Principle or the 80/20 Rule? Italian economist Vilfredo Pareto made an observation in the early 1900s that 80 per cent of Italy's wealth was owned by 20 per cent of its population. He subsequently observed other economies and found similar distributions of wealth. He published his findings in his first work, *Cours d'économie politique* (1896–1897). Pareto never took his findings much further, but in the early 1950s quality management pioneer Dr Joseph Juran published his *Quality Control Handbook* and in it he spoke of the principle that he called the Law of the Vital Few. Dr Juran's observation of the "vital few" was based around the principle that 20 per cent of something is always responsible for 80 per cent of the results. His theory intended to apply Pareto's observations of wealth to quality losses and henceforth became known as the Pareto Principle or the 80/20 Rule.

It was widely assumed that Juran was applying Pareto's economic principle to a broader field. Pareto's observations were concerned with the distribution of the wealth of a nation, while Juran's initial studies were based on quality management and his observations that 20 per cent of defects caused 80 per cent of problems. But Juran found that this 80/20 phenomenon could be applied to a myriad of subjects and it is now a widely recognised model in the world of business.

Examples of the Pareto Principle include:

In the business world:

- 80 per cent of your revenue comes from 20 per cent of your clients.
- 80 per cent of your business activity comes from 20 per cent of your employees.
- 80 per cent of your sales come from 20 per cent of your products.
- 80 per cent of your storage is taken up by 20 per cent of your stock.
- 80 per cent of your stock comes from 20 per cent of your suppliers.

In your personal life:

- 80 per cent of your time is spent with 20 per cent of your acquaintances.
- 20 per cent of your clothes you wear 80 per cent of the time.
- 20 per cent of your recipes you use 80 per cent of the time.

In the world of productivity:

- 20 per cent of what you do gives you 80 per cent of the results!

Applying the Pareto Principle

When this principle is applied to our working day, we can see that very often time is not the issue, but prioritisation. So when we look at the Pareto Principle and apply it to productivity, we very often find that only 20 per cent of the work that we do is important; 80 per cent of our activities are activities that could either be eliminated or be done by someone else.

It is necessary to stop and analyse the current picture before we start to make changes and improvements. Have you ever had one of those days where, come 5.00 p.m., you can't figure out what you have spent the last eight hours doing? In productivity terms this is not a desirable situation to find yourself in, but don't worry – it is a common phenomenon. To work at your best you need to first figure out how you are presently passing the hours and then you can start to plan the time more constructively.

First, you need to be aware of how your time is being spent; then you identify your important 20 per cent. Which activities are the critical activities and which are the ones that add little or no value to your goals or to the goals of your organisation? By focusing on the important 20 per cent we can get our desired results faster and with less effort. The next exercise is about identifying and focusing on this 20 per cent or what Juran coined "the vital few":

Step 1: Write down the top ten activities that take up your time in a working day.
Step 2: Put a percentage on each of these items according to how much time they take up each day.
Step 3: Write down the top two most important aspects of your job, i.e. the parts of your job that add most value to your organisation.
Step 4: Put a percentage on each of these items according to how much time you spend on these items daily.

Are you starting to see how your time is being spent?

To get an even more accurate idea of how your time is being spent, it is useful to create a timesheet. Detail all the tasks that you complete in a day and the time spent on each activity. Write in start and stop times for each activity. Try and be as detailed as possible, noting time spent chatting to colleagues, toilet breaks, coffee breaks and any other activities that take up your time. At the end of the day add up all the time spent on each category: surfing the web, administration, phone calls, etc. At the end of one week you should get a good picture of how your days are being spent.

This task can be a time-consuming process but a very valuable analysis. There is a much faster and more effective alternative for the lazy amongst us – an electronic timesheet. Log onto www.officemetrics.com where you can download a free personal edition of OfficeMetrics, a personal productivity tool, which can show you exactly how you spend your time on your computer. It details the documents used, and time spent reading and writing emails, surfing the net, on the telephone, at meetings, and so on.

You will be amazed at how much time you waste even when you think you are having a productive day. Studies have shown that the average office worker is only productive 1.5 hours a day. Shocking, isn't it? The rest of the time is spent socialising, doing irrelevant tasks and being interrupted by co-workers.

Elimination

Eliminating the unnecessary tasks that take up our time is the next step. Author Timothy Ferriss follows this principle to the extreme, the result of which has led him to something we would all aspire to – the four-hour work week. In his book, aptly titled *The 4-Hour Workweek*, he claims that so much of our time is spent doing tasks that are neither profitable nor beneficial to our organisation, and that a lot of the tasks that need doing could be done by others at a much cheaper rate.

Ferriss suggests some interesting questions to get us thinking about the vital work and therefore helping us to see what tasks can be eliminated or passed on to someone else. For example, if you were to have a heart attack and could only work two hours per day, what would you do? Or if you could only complete one task today, what would it be? These questions allow us to eliminate the unessential and focus on what is really required. If you are lucky enough to have someone to whom you can delegate work, go ahead and delegate. Remember what Edsger Dijkstra said: "Only do what only you can do."

Focus on your goals

As you try to eliminate tasks that are not giving you results, have your goals as your focus. Ask yourself: Is this activity taking me closer to my goals? If the answer is no, eliminate it; if it is yes, take a look and see if there is a more efficient way to complete this task or if it is necessary for you personally to complete it. The trick is to work on only what really matters. We fill our lives doing work that we think has to be done. Why do we do this? One reason is that society has told us that we must be busy between 9.00 a.m. and 5.00 p.m. each day and, if we are not, it means we aren't being productive enough. Another reason why we keep filling our lives with work is to avoid the tasks that we are uncomfortable with, the ones that take us out of our comfort zone. We keep going back to our email and choosing the next task that is easiest and most fun over the ones that may be confrontational or may require a lot of work to complete.

As I was writing this book, I eliminated a lot of my usual activities in order to free up time to be able to complete it in the time frame I had set for myself. When I started to write the book, I was busy with work tasks and I was also studying. I had many goals and responsibilities and, yes, at times I would become overwhelmed and frustrated that I wasn't getting as much work done as I would have liked. So I simplified things. I decided to focus on my studies and complete them; once I had that done, I would focus on the book. Sometimes it is possible to have a single focus but other times we don't have that luxury. This single focus was powerful in aiding the book's completion, but the biggest thing that helped was that I did away with so many activities that would normally take up some of my time. I significantly reduced the time I spent on the web. I eliminated Facebook, LinkedIn and Twitter. I stopped reading newsletters, news-papers and magazines. I stopped watching television. I had to make my choices and I did this by focusing on my biggest and most important goal, which was to finish and publish this book.

The social media explosion has rocked the world of productivity. It saps time from the unsuspecting, but, on the flipside, it can eliminate hundreds of hours of research and networking for those working in sales and marketing. Depending on how you use it, it can be a saint or a devil. If you are falling into the social networking arena be sure that the time you are investing in your online marketing strategy is paying off. Like everything else, the awareness of how you spend your time online, and what its rewards are, are critical to avoiding wasting thousands of hours yearly.

Originally, Juran's Law of the Vital Few was known as the Law of the Vital Few and the Trivial Many, but Juran in later years preferred the Law of the Vital Few and the Important Many. We have to be careful not to eliminate all activities that fall into the 80 per cent, as not all of these are time-wasting activities. The trick is to eliminate the useless but also to start to schedule time for the important and less important tasks, or to delegate and outsource the tasks that don't need to be carried out by you.

Plan and schedule

Once you have eliminated the tasks that you have identified as unnecessary or transferable to another person, you need to schedule time for the tasks that need to be done. There are some daily tasks that are crucial and must be done regardless of interruptions. Take the example of payroll – this job must be done on a certain day at a certain time. If this was your responsibility and the job wasn't done on time, do you think your life would be worth living?

Analyse your responsibilities and decide which items come under this category. Obviously these are the first to call your attention.

The infamous words of Peter Druker have to be mentioned: "Fail to plan, plan to fail." Planning the work that needs to be done and when it is going to get done is crucial. You will see how your productivity will escalate if you begin to schedule your tasks. Establishing a routine of planning your work will be a habit you never regret. Use a diary, calendar or electronic calendar, such as the one in Microsoft Outlook or Lotus Notes.

Once a week, take some time and plan out the work that needs to be done for the week. This should include any personal commitments. As David Allen, the author of *Getting Things Done*, says: Anything that needs to be done can be defined as work, including organising children's parties or redecorating a room. Anything that takes more than thirty minutes to complete should be allocated time in the calendar. Tasks that get scheduled get done. Never fill your schedule completely because, as the saying goes, "Stuff Happens!" You will never know what new priorities may come your way in a week. Leave a 30–40 per cent contingency. This you will be able to judge for yourself as time goes on. If you find that 30–40 per cent is never enough, then you may have to look again at the tasks you are scheduling or the unplanned work that is coming your way. Is it your responsibility? Can it be done by someone else? Can it be ignored or eliminated altogether?

What happens if your best customer interrupts the important project you are working on and that you have two hours scheduled for? Well, of course you have no choice but to attend to him or her, but remember to return to your task when you are finished, even if your client has asked you to do something for them. The best tactic is to schedule the new task into your daily planner. It is better to advise your customer that the task will be done tomorrow rather than today, and that you have other urgent work to complete first. If the customer's request is more urgent than your current project, reschedule the project and complete the task for your customer.

Interruptions are part of life, and making decisions regarding priorities happens daily. The important thing to remember is to reschedule the tasks that get thrown out due to the interruption, while always keeping your eyes on the goal.

Your organisational style

Apart from knowing what you are currently spending your time on, it is also important to know your personal work style. In the book *How to Be Organised in Spite of Yourself*, Sunny Schlenger and Roberta Roesch list five different organisational styles regarding time management and five styles for space management.

You may be a "hopper" or "allergic to detail"; you could be an "everything out" or a "total slob", but by knowing your natural tendency, you can use the correct remedy to counteract any bad habits or personality characteristics that may prevent you from being as productive as you should be.

Awareness includes both understanding yourself and your work style and the knowledge of how your time is currently being spent. Without this awareness you cannot hope to maximise your productivity potential. Having this awareness will bring you one step closer to being the best you can be.

Productivity tips from Section 2 – Awareness

1. Start using a time sheet to help you see how you are currently spending your time.

2. Employ the Pareto Principle and try to identify your important 20 per cent.

3. Eliminate any activities that aren't helping your get closer to your goals.

4. Find out your organisational style and work with it.

5. Schedule your tasks – they are much more likely to get done that way.

section 3 – systems

4

getting ready for action

clearing the path for success

"Simplicity is making the journey of this
life with just baggage enough."

– Author Unknown

Many people will tell you productivity systems don't work,
but these are the same people who say that diets or the gym
don't help you to lose weight. Systems work when you
implement them correctly and use them regularly. Once you
commit to putting in a bit of hard work at the implementation stage, you will reap the benefits far into the future.

The reason why systems work is that they take the decisions and reasoning out of the equation. With a system,
we don't have to spend time thinking and debating what
we should do; we can just go ahead and do it. Without the
element of reasoning, we can move on more quickly to the
next phase: *action*.

The benefits of having a system

Weight Watchers is a weight-loss system that works for
millions of people all over the world. People follow instructions on how to measure what they eat daily. The combination

of different food types such as protein, carbohydrates and fats are converted into "points". The dieter then counts the number of points they have consumed in a day. They are only allowed to consume a certain number of points, but earn extra points for exercise. Weight Watchers gives them guidance and manuals that help them to work out and track the points in all foods that they eat. The people who do Weight Watchers diets don't eat properly every day of their diet; a lot make mistakes and a lot fall off the wagon. But the beauty of the Weight Watchers system is that it allows for this and it encourages you to get back on track. By knowing and understanding your system, any delay in getting back on track is minimised.

I have recently lost weight using the Weight Watchers system. The leader at the class I attend spoke some very powerful words one week when he said, "You are all going to fall down. That doesn't matter. What matters is how long you stay lying down." If we can embrace this concept for weight loss, getting organised or any positive habit we wish to create, we are less likely to fall into the negative self-criticising mind-set which can ultimately lead to failure to complete our goals. If we have a system to fall back on, we are much more likely to have success with our goals.

So, where do we start?

When people want to learn to become more productive and organised they are often at a loss as to where to start. The task appears overwhelming and they cannot see the big picture because the disorder and untidiness have clouded their vision and clarity. So some come looking for help and ask, "How can I become organised? I need to focus more – how can I work more effectively?"

Rest assured, there are answers and solutions to every stressful and disorganised work environment. With the right tools, designed for the particular place of work, anyone or any organisation can become more organised, more productive and more relaxed.

We start with clearing the clutter, and shedding the mind of thoughts, the inbox of emails and the desk of papers.

Emptying your mind and clearing your environment can help you to focus. Feng shui experts will tell you that clutter is a sign of stuck, stagnant energy, and the negative effect this can have on different areas of your life can be enormous. The location of the clutter in your life can directly influence the flow of events in that particular area. Followers of Zen Buddhism will advise of the power of simplicity, letting go of all baggage, and focusing on the here and now. Focusing on the present moment is very difficult if you are carrying clutter, whether physical or emotional. For this reason, clearing the clutter is an essential step in the process and one of the most powerful productivity tools I can advocate. Never underestimate the effect that disorder can have on your psyche.

Phase 1 – de-clutter

It is difficult to work on your vision and goals with clarity if your day-to-day activities are chaotic and disorganised. The best place to start de-cluttering is your immediate environment – your personal living space and your personal workspace. The house and the office are the more urgent areas to tackle as these are the spaces you occupy daily, and it is crucial for stress-free productivity and focus that these areas are free from distractions.

The personal environment

Begin by dumping all the unnecessary things in your house.

Ask yourself the following questions:

- Is it useful?
- Is it beautiful?
- Have I used it/worn it in the past twelve months?

There may be items such as beach wear or ski wear that you haven't worn in the past year but that you want to hold on to. This is fine, but if after twenty-four months you still haven't used them, it may be time to consider throwing them out or giving them away.

Start small and de-clutter in small bites: maybe take one room at a time or, if this is too much, one drawer or cupboard at a time. Set a time and schedule some space in your calendar or diary for the task. You will feel a great sense of achievement when it is done.

You can also consider giving yourself a time goal, if a room or area is too overwhelming. For example, spend one hour on Saturday clearing out the guest room. When the hour is up, be proud of your achievement and schedule another hour on another day.

Before you start:

- Buy refuse sacks.
- Buy storage boxes.
- Find out where the local charity shop is.

Recently my husband and I saw a house that we were interested in buying, and we were both very excited about the prospect of a move. The thing I was most excited about was the feeling of a fresh start. I began to imagine clearing my wardrobe of all the things that I really did not need in preparation for the move – the expensive clothes that I have kept but don't fit me anymore, the shoes that match only one outfit, the handbags that are so out of fashion my mother wouldn't use them, and the twenty-three pairs of gloves and thirty hats that I was keeping in case of a really cold winter! In the end, we decided that we weren't going to make the move but the desire to clear my space didn't go away.

I am not a hoarder – I live in a small townhouse with no attic and three children so I don't have the space to store stuff. However, I regularly have enough stuff to fill my car for the charity shop and I could probably go more often if I was ruthless enough. Being like a magpie is not good for humans' well-being.

Obstacles to clearing the path

There are many reasons why people like to hold on to things they no longer need:

1. It can be difficult to throw out something that has cost a lot of money.
2. Sentimentality or emotional reasons. For example:

   - You can't accept you'll never fit into those clothes again.
   - You won't admit that you will never use your sports equipment again.
   - You can't detach yourself from the objects of a deceased family member.
   - You are reluctant to face the fact that children have moved on and won't be coming back.

3. A hatred of waste.
4. Procrastination or a lack of discipline.

As you can see, the existence of clutter is not quite as simple as pure procrastination. So how do we overcome these factors?

As with all problems, the first step is awareness. If you start to clear out an area of your house and you begin to feel very uncomfortable, stop and analyse the reason for this. Be honest with yourself and spend some time thinking about the reasons. Take your time but also realise that holding on to things that in reality are no longer a part of your life is only creating a barrier between you and the life you should be living.

> Clearing the clutter will allow more space for the right things to enter your life.

Here are some points to remember that may help you to say goodbye.

The real value of objects – out with the old

We must realise that items don't hold their value regardless of the amount of money that was paid for them.

If you are holding onto items you don't use because you spent a lot of money on them at the time, you have to rationalise that no matter how up-to-the-minute or top-of-the-range some items are, unfortunately they are not worth much a couple of years later. So, if you have one of the first mobile phones released hidden away in your cupboard – the type used by Michael Douglas in the original *Wall Street* film – it's time to fish it out and say goodbye.

Technology or electronics don't hold their value because within twelve months something new and better has come on to the market.

Ask yourself these questions:

- Do I have any use for this item?
- Have I used it in the last twelve months?

- Is there anyone I know who can make use of it? (Maybe you can avail of a bartering system.)
- Could I donate the object to charity?
- Could I sell the item on eBay and make some money from it?

Emotional reasons – hanging on too long

There are also all kinds of emotional reasons we hang onto "stuff", but it is necessary to become aware of the reasons and try to move forwards. Impractical fears can prevent us from moving forwards with our lives.

I spent a number of years living in Spain, where my friends regularly went skiing or snowboarding. I decided to join in the fun and go snowboarding with them. I found it very difficult, but I loved it all the same and loved the image associated with it, the freedom and courage that it represented for me. When I moved back home, I brought my snowboard with me. It sat in the corner (on display) for rather a long time for everyone to see that I was "a snowboarder"! I took a trip to Andorra one year and had a wild and exciting week with a spout of concussion thrown in for good measure. After that holiday, I realised the following:

- I wasn't very good at snowboarding.
- It was quite an unrealistic hobby since I lived in a country without snow.
- If I did want to go again, I could hire the equipment.

The logic of all of these factors didn't prevent my heart from breaking as the woman who bought my board, boots and bag walked out my front door! There have been times when I looked back and regretted selling them, but I knew that something better would come along to occupy my time and space.

Sentimentality – hanging on to too much

Sentimentality is understandable and holding on to keep-sakes from our parents or ancestors is nice, but there is a limit to their value in our lives.

I'm not suggesting you must throw out sentimental memorabilia or all photos from the past, but there must be a limit to how much the past controls our lives. Living in the present means we don't allow the past to run our lives. We cannot change the past, but we do have the ability to change and affect the present.

There is usually another emotional or psychological reason for this kind of hoarding, but it is a habit that must be broken. Yes, we learn from our past but if we cannot let go of it we are blocking current and future possibilities from entering our lives. Letting go is one of the quickest ways to reach our goals.

In the words of Omar Khayyam:[4]

Ah my beloved, fill the cup that clears
To-day of past Regrets and Future Fears:
To-morrow, why To-morrow I may be
Myself with yesterday's seven Thousand Years.

Ah fill the cup what boots it to repeat
How time is slipping underneath our Feet.
Unborn To-morrow and dead Yesterday
Why fret about them if To-day be sweet.

Hate waste?

A very practical way to overcome fear of waste is to recycle or donate objects to charity. Most cities and towns have charity

---

[4] Translated by Edward Fitzgerald, from *The Golden Treasury of the Best Songs and Lyrical Poems in the English Language*, Oxford: Oxford University Press, 1950.

shops that will take a lot of your objects off your hands. Another possible way to offload, as mentioned, is eBay, the website where one man's waste is another man's gold!

Procrastination

Procrastination – to adjourn for tomorrow what could be done today – is perhaps the antithesis of productivity. Some like to lean on the word as if it is an acceptable crutch to adopt. The reasons for procrastination are many:

- Underlying beliefs that we hold
- Fear of the outcome
- Overwhelming size of a task
- Lack of organisation
- Sheer laziness

Refer to Section 6 – Enemies to Focus, for ways to overcome procrastination.

Phase 2 – the working environment

So, after we have cleared unnecessary objects from our home, we must then look at our workspace and desk.

Schedule some time in your calendar to clear out your office:

1. Make sure you have a good filing system and, if you decide you are going to keep something for reference, file it away. Go through your files and filing cabinets and throw out anything that you no longer need. If you already have an electronic copy or if you can easily get something again don't hold onto it (unless they are documents you are required to keep by law).

2. Never mix documents that need to be filed for reference with your work that still needs to be done. It makes your work to do appear to be more than it is and can affect you negatively.

3. Go through your drawers and throw out anything you do not use on a regular basis. Get desk organisers, in-trays and file stands for your desk.

There are many books written offering detailed systems for dealing with your personal organisation and workflow. Perhaps the most well known and my personal favourite is David Allen's *Getting Things Done.* (See Section 3 – Workflow Systems for more details.)

De-clutter your computer

Most of us use our computer for most of our day, so ensuring that you have it organised in an efficient manner will also be a great advantage when it comes to getting things done quickly and efficiently.

Manage your files correctly

Start by creating a filing system if you don't already have one. Create folders for all your main areas of work, and then create subfolders inside them to represent the different areas. Try and keep it simple as over-complicating things will find you still searching for your documents after organising them too neatly and efficiently!

Delete old documents

Most people hold on to too many files, the rationale being "I have the space so I may as well keep them in case I need them in the future." Nine point nine times out of ten, you won't require the files in the future, but that has to be your call. Consider backing up your work on an external hard drive. Once you have done this, you will no longer need to store stuff on your own computer. This will free up space, making the computer faster, and easier to navigate and find what you are looking for.

Avoid the desktop

Countless people have the bad habit of saving everything on their desktop for easy retrieval. It may appear to be a good idea for productivity, but the problem arises when you save too much to the desktop. When you save to your desktop, you are saving into your user profile, and if your user profile gets too big you will risk corrupting files, thus meaning you could lose important data. System restore in Microsoft Windows does not always restore all desktop files. It is better to store your files in a logical manner, either on your hard drive or on a network server for security. If you really like using your desktop, best practice is to create a shortcut to a folder, rather than saving the file itself to the desktop.

Check out other tips in Section 4 – Technology to help make your computer run faster and more efficiently.

Phase 3 – your mind

How to clear your mind

Yes, you guessed it – the first step to clearing your mind is making a list. By getting it down on paper you are downloading the responsibility from your mind. Call it the Mind Dump, the Mind Sweep or whatever name works for you; just get it out of your head.

When doing the Mind Sweep, it is important to remember that spelling, formatting and sectioning are not important. Some people can't help themselves and even after they have been told to create a random list, they will instinctively begin to create headings and place the stuff from their mind in neatly organised sections. This is not the goal. When we dump or download what's on our mind, we want to do so in the fastest possible manner – everything from collecting clothes from the dry cleaners to starting a new project, or maybe buying new payroll software. Let no thought escape the process. You are creating an "unkempt to-do list", a list where current and future tasks go side by side with a wish list and a list of unlimited possibilities.

Once we have cleared the mind of our tasks and duties, what do we do with this information?

We organise the items to be done into our system. So if an item needs to be done on Friday, you will put it into your diary or calendar for Friday. If there are things that have to be done today we put that in our today's list of things to do. The Getting Things Done method suggests that we no longer have a generic to-do list but that we categorise our to-do list in order to do similar tasks together at the same time, which allows us to focus more on the task we are currently doing and not feel overwhelmed by all the other things that still need to be done. You can create a notebook for this or use Microsoft Outlook or a similar email program, which has the facility to categorise tasks. This can be very useful as you can synchronise your smartphone so that you have your task list with you at all times.

An hour after I did my first Mind Sweep, I left the house to go and collect a family member from the airport. It was a summer's day and I felt great. As I drove, I started to feel a little elated. I kept thinking of past summers when I had just completed my end-of-year school or college exams. I couldn't figure out why these images kept coming into my mind until I realised the emotion I was feeling could be likened to that end-of-term feeling of freedom, completion, lightness and no responsibility.

How could this be so if I still had a big workload at home? None of the work had been done, but I had identified all the work that needed to be done. My mind was free from clutter; I was in control of my workload it was no longer controlling me. Every time I tell someone that getting organised is a life-changing phenomenon they think I exaggerate, but believe me, when you begin to clear your mind, your desk and your environment, the feeling of being in control is so relaxing and powerful it can't but change your life for the better.

5

minimalism

a journey in simplicity

"Everything should be made as simple as possible, but not simpler."

– Albert Einstein

Living as a minimalist can work very well for some people. The minimalist tries to simplify their life by limiting their possessions and decomplicating the way in which they live their life. The minimalist chooses their diet of information and property well. Only the essential and important are allowed to enter their life. I have always said that happiness lies in simplicity, and the more I explore minimalism the more truth I see in this statement.

Our lives in the Western World are submerged in advertising and marketing. TV and the internet have become integrated into our lives at a cellular level. Our brains are changing and adapting to the constant input. Children expect and crave high levels of stimulation. Every click, every link will lead us to an array of objects that we yearn for, desire, crave – mostly things we don't actually need. For example, how many pairs of shoes does a person need? I look in my cupboard and I find hiking boots, hiking shoes, running shoes, tennis runners, casual runners, brown work shoes, black work shoes, brown boots, black boots, flip-flops and sandals (and that's just to start with). A lot of people will relate to this list and even more people will actually have more shoes than that. Is it sufficient? Should it be sufficient? Can we eliminate and reduce the abundance of stuff that has taken over our lives.

On a recent trip to South Africa, I was reminded again of the surplus of wealth that we have in the Western World. In South Africa, it's quite possible for a family of ten to live in a space that we would deem too small for our garden shed. I saw young boys in the shanty towns playing football with a woven ball of plastic bags, and I felt embarrassed when I thought of the ten balls of different shapes and sizes that my kids own.

Not only can our legacy of abundance be seen as repugnant, as it adds to the destruction of the very elements that feed us and keep us alive. The overproduction of goods that marketers convince us we need is destroying our planet. Industry contributes to the depletion of our planet's natural resources and is responsible for polluting our air, rivers and seas. This profusion of stuff has cluttered our immediate environments, and is causing havoc with our minds and our spirits (see the previous chapter for a discussion of the impact of clutter on our lives).

My aim is not to depress you but to awaken you to the futility of acquiring more and more and more. Rather than going shopping at the weekend, ask yourself what other pastime you would really like to pursue, that you claim you never have time for.

What exactly is minimalism?

Many people have preconceptions of what minimalism is. They believe you can't own a car or a house and have to limit yourself to a number of possessions. This may be true for some minimalists but minimalism has no concrete rules. The concept of minimalism is about freedom; it is a tool for stripping away the unnecessary so that you can focus on the essentials and ultimately live a happier more meaningful life.

Leo Babauta, the writer of the blog Zen Habits, describes minimalism as follows:

> "It's a way to escape the excesses of the world around us — the excesses of consumerism, material possessions, clutter, having too much to do, too much debt, too many distractions, too much noise. But too little meaning. Minimalism is a way of eschewing the non-essential in order to focus on what's truly important, what gives our lives meaning, what gives us joy and value."

You can read more on Leo's minimalist blog at http://mnmlist.com.

Joshua Becker, who writes the Becoming Minimalist blog, explains what minimalism means to him:

> "I am intentionally trying to live with only the things that I really need."

For a more in-depth explanation from Joshua, go to http://becomingminimalist.com.

Minimalism is a potent productivity tool; it allows for elimination of physical and psychic clutter, a recipe for productivity disaster. It reduces distraction; it fosters focus; it is the very essence of what we are striving for with productivity enhancement: control, simplicity and stress-free efficiency.

Benefits of minimalism

There are many benefits of minimalism and, as every minimalist chooses to live his or her life in accordance to what is important to them, these benefits will vary. I have included some of the most common.

You have more *time* because you:

- Spend less time shopping and no longer buy unnecessary items
- Spend less time cleaning and dusting due to fewer objects and furniture
- Have fewer possessions to look after and clean
- Spend less time reading unnecessary information
- Reduce your emails by unsubscribing to newsletters

You have more *money* because you:

- Spend less money on unnecessary things
- Become more conscious about how you spend money
- Use less electricity by being more conscious of standby power
- Walk when possible instead of driving, reducing money spent on petrol or diesel

You are *doing good* by:

- Caring for the environment through generating less waste
- Reducing your carbon footprint by walking when possible
- Being an example to your children

Embracing minimalism

To embrace the concept of minimalism, you need to start by eliminating that which is not essential from your life.

Using the ideas from Section 2, begin to reduce your possessions and limit what you allow to enter your life. Minimalism in your physical environment can help you to live a simpler, more fulfilling life by allowing you to focus on what really matters.

6

workflow systems

organising your world of work

> "Your mind is for having ideas, not
> holding them."

> – David Allen

You may hear people speaking about workflow systems. Workflow management systems are ways in which you can organise yourself and your workload to work more efficiently and get more done in a day, without adding more stress.

We need workflow systems because people are rarely trained in how to approach their workload. Workers are hardly ever instructed into a workflow or email management protocol. They are seldom shown how to maintain and store their documents. They are expected to know how to deal with their excessive emails and electronic files. Our information workers are lacking a vital ingredient to enable them to be skilled efficient workers. They need to learn how to go about doing their work. In short, they need a system.

What if we don't implement a system?

Poor personal productivity can lead to lack of task completion, unmet deadlines, the need to work longer hours, unreturned emails and stress. Many information workers suffer from some if not all of the above scenarios. For an organisation, poor productivity can lead to financial losses for the company through reduced work performance, stress-related absences and loss of sales due to poor customer service.

Some individuals are more effective than others at completing their weekly tasks, but by improving personal productivity and personal workflow systems everyone can free up time and energy to focus on the big picture, and spend more time innovating, and on creative thinking and problem solving. By putting simple workflow systems in place, these symptoms of poor personal productivity can be tackled and eliminated.

Workflow systems have been devised to help people to manage their workflow (the way in which you do your work). One of the best and most well know workflow system is that of David Allen – the Getting Things Done (GTD) methodology.

Getting Things Done

David Allen's methodology is based on two key principles:

1. Capturing everything that needs to get done into a logical system outside of your head

2. Disciplining yourself to make front-end decisions with your work so that you always have a plan for the next action that needs to be completed, in order to be able to get your work done efficiently

In his book *Getting Things Done*, Allen teaches a process called "The Five Stages of Mastering Workflow". He says there are five distinct stages we go through when dealing with our work. They are: 1. Collection, 2. Processing, 3. Organising,

4. Reviewing and 5. Doing. He says that most people use a process that includes some of these stages, but if you miss out any one of these stages, or if you chose to do something before you have ascertained if it is the best thing to do at that moment, you won't maximise the potential of the system.

The five stages

1. Collection

The collection process involves the gathering together of what Allen calls "open loops" – anything in your life that still needs to be done. These can be household tasks or work projects. Anything that you need to or want to do should be collected in some sort of basket, tray or location for processing and sorting. These tools are only as good as you make them so it is no use having a physical in-basket if you still leave papers lying around on different desks. You must be disciplined enough to use your collection tools. Try to have as many as you need but as few as possible – too many places to collect will complicate your system. I have come across many people who have removed their voicemail function from their phone to eliminate having to check on voicemails. If you wish to follow suit, put a message on your voicemail which says something like the following: "Please don't leave a message. If you need to contact me urgently, call again later or send an email to the following address…"

An important part of the collection process is to collect everything that is in your head. So doing a Mind Dump or a Mind Sweep would be useful here. Take a piece of paper or a note in Microsoft Outlook and start to put down all of the items that need to get done in your life. Once you have collected all the work that needs doing, the next step is to process it.

2. Processing

The processing phase is deciding what needs to be done with what you have collected. Processing and organising are done before the work starts. The mistake a lot of people make is to actually try to do the work before it is processed and organised. The processing phase is the decision time, when you ask the questions what is this and what am I going to do with it?

3. Organising

There are many ways in which you can organise your work, but a calendar and a task reminder list are essential. There are many task management software programs with which to store your task lists, for example, Remember The Milk and Wunderlist. Free calendars can be found online or in your email program. Google Calendar is popular. Allen recommends categorising the elements of the to-do list so that we can group our work in certain areas. So if you need to make a couple of phone calls, you can create a category called "Phone". Other categories could be created for emails that need to be sent, for work that needs to be done at home and for work at the computer, etc.

Documents or electronic work that needs to be kept for reference should be stored in a logical filing system. There are a few important points to consider when creating a physical filing system. If your filing cabinet is in an awkward place, you are unlikely to do your filing as often as it should be done. Having a filing cabinet in close proximity to your desk will make it more accessible and user friendly. Create a simple A–Z filing system; don't complicate it with subsections. Buy lots of folders and keep them close at hand so they are available when you need to create a new folder for something. Keep the drawers of your filing cabinet less than three-quarters full; if they are too full you will be more reluctant to do your filing and it will be more difficult to find the files when you are looking for them. Label all your folders with a labeller. At first I didn't see the necessity of using a labeller but when I started to use it I realised the benefits, as finding files is now a painless process.

4. Reviewing

The reviewing phase – looking back over your calendar and task lists to ensure what needed to get done got done – or a weekly review is essential to the efficient working of the system. At review time you should gather and process all your work, review all areas of your system, update your lists and make sure everything is current and up to date.

5. Doing

As stated by Allen in *Getting Things Done*: "The basic purpose of the workflow-management process is to facilitate good choices about what you're doing at any point in time." To enable the correct decision for choosing what action to take at a given time, he used The Four-Criteria Model for Choosing Actions in the Moment. The Four Criteria are:

a. Context

b. Time available

c. Energy available

d. Priority

Here I have given a very basic outline of my view of what the GTD system is about. It is a system that works. Many people feel overwhelmed by the detail of his system, but this is the reason why it works so well. There is a solution for every situation we find ourselves in. Implementing the system was one of the best things I did for my personal productivity, and my life as a whole. It transformed the way I think about work and about my life in general. It has facilitated many of my achievements and successes. It did what it claimed to do and allowed me to enter a state of stress-free productivity.

Productivity tips from Section 3 – Systems

1. De-clutter your environment, home, office, mind and PC.
2. Consider the benefits of minimalism – live life in a more simple way.
3. Adopt a workflow system, such as the Getting Things Done method.
4. Implement a good, simple filing system so that you can find your documents.
5. Review your system weekly to make sure everything continues to get done.

section 4 – technology

7

computer systems

the world in which we live

"I do not fear computers. I fear the lack of them."

– Isaac Asimov

Investment in information and communications technology is fundamental to raising levels of efficiency. IT can improve business processes and speed up existing procedures. It would also be advisable to regularly assess the current systems being used to ensure there are no areas causing delays in the company workflow. By doing this and by considering the future requirements of the company, we can gauge the necessity of improvements in both hardware and software.

It could also help in an individual capacity to take an objective look at the systems and equipment you are using and assess if they are meeting your requirements and serving your needs.

Technological infrastructure may just be the competitive edge you need. Minutes saved daily though efficient use of technology add up to hours monthly and weeks yearly. My brother-in-law is a scientist, whose research leads the field in cutting-edge technology that may just transform the world as we know it today. One of his concerns is that his team is working as efficiently and as productively as it possibly can, because, for him, these minutes, hours and weeks could cost him a Nobel prize for science!

Hardware

So, what needs to be considered to ensure that your technology is not slowing you down? Perhaps an investment in hardware may be necessary?

Desktops and laptops: Old PCs can be slow. If your PC takes five minutes to boot up each day, do you know how much time are you wasting in a year? Almost four working days! Desktops and laptops are not expensive pieces of equipment. It is advisable to update them regularly. The faster your PC the quicker you can complete your work. Different job roles will require different specifications. If you are an administrator who only uses Microsoft Office programs, you will not require as much speed and processing power as a computer programmer who will depend on processing power to compile their software.

Printers and scanners: If you or your workers are sharing a printer or a scanner, is this slowing down workflow? How much time do you/they spend waiting for the printer to be free? Do the maths for this one and multiply the hourly rate by the time wasted, and then compare with the cost of a new printer. I once worked for a company that had two network printers, which were 200 metres and 400 metres respectively from my desk. Every time I had a requirement to print, I had to leave my office to collect the printouts. Each time I left my office there was the possibility of me being distracted by colleagues or the lure of the cafeteria. On occasions when the printer didn't print my document, I had to go back to my office to check out the problem. It would have saved that company a lot of money in labour time to install a printer in the office I shared with three others.

Business phones: Smart phones are not just for checking email and updating Twitter. They can be synched with your work computer, allowing you to download your address book, calendar, task list and notes to your phone. In this way you do not need to duplicate address books or keep a paper diary or calendar. Smart phones are advancing daily as all technology is, but with the myriad of iPhone or Android apps available, it is phenomenal the amount of tasks that we can complete much faster and more efficiently with a smart phone. Many workers use their phones for keeping expense accounts, to-do lists, currency converters, language translators, conference calling and many other functions. The danger, as with all technology, is that the phone becomes a distraction or a time waster. The wisest way to avoid this as a company is to create a phone template or protocol for what the phone should be used for. As an individual, one can check out blogs and other resources online to get advice on which apps or programs are the best and can add value to each individual's or company's requirements.

Networks and servers: Ensure networks are sufficiently fast and aren't causing delays; again, speed of hardware used can have a major effect on work efficiency.

Internet access: Speed is of the essence here. Is the broadband sufficiently fast to avoid bottlenecks? Research the best speeds available and make sure you are connected.

Back-up: Do you have a dedicated back-up drive? Regular back-ups are essential to working in a relaxed and efficient manner. If you were to lose all your current data, how long would it take you to recreate it? Would you be able to? Would you still have a business if you lost your data? This is a risk so many people take; countless people daily lose their hard drives and don't have a back-up in place. Installing a company back-up system is one of the first things you should think of after purchasing your first computer. If you are an individual, a simple external hard drive can be picked up in any computer store and they are relatively inexpensive. Factor this cost into your budget for a computer or laptop. You don't want to lose all your precious family photos or videos.

Software

If the hardware you possess is up to date, maybe the software systems you run are outdated and could be improved?

Customer management databases: Customer relationship management (CRM) software or any other type of customer database can be used by many different departments for different purposes. Make sure that your software packages are not overlapping and that one system would not suffice for two or three or all departments. On the other hand, the requirements for different departments may be so diverse that forcing a triangle into a square hole will not be the cleverest move for the overall organisation. A scenario analysis of departmental requirements will determine the overall software requirement.

Open source software: Check out open source software such as openoffice.org. A friend just saved €50,000 on Microsoft licences by moving his company to OpenOffice and Google Apps for Business. A small amount of training was required to familiarise workers with the new software, but the savings made it well worthwhile. Applications like Google Apps or

Microsoft 365 can help increase productivity right across the organisation as workers can access their data from anywhere they can use the internet.

Email programs: Investigate your email programs and make sure you are using them fully. The majority of people use just 20 per cent of an email program's capabilities and don't use calendars, task lists and the other functions that they provide. An email program can be used as a simple CRM if all customer contact details are kept up to date. Every time you receive a business card, details should be entered into the address book and the business card dumped! When syncing your phone with your computer, the contact details will be copied to the necessary location, ensuring that your address book is current. The calendar function of an email program should be used to schedule all tasks that need to be undertaken. All items that need to be done at a specific time or on a particular date, or any item that is going to take you longer than thirty minutes to complete should be given a calendar slot.

Intranets: An intranet is a company's internal network interfaced with HTML or web technology. Simple navigation links can make an intranet one of the most effective internal communication systems that can be used. A clear, well-designed intranet can reduce an employee's searching time on the network by hours weekly. It is also a very effective way to train new workers; they orientate themselves much faster and start to be productive much sooner. A further benefit is that of effective internal communications. An organisation can update company news and product changes regularly, which keeps employees informed at all times.

I was once contracted by a company who had four separate databases recording different information about the same clients. Some clients would appear in all databases and some clients would only appear in one. They started out with one DOS-based database (an operating system originally developed for IBM personal computers) which was more than sufficient for their requirements at the outset of their business. But as the business grew and their products and services expanded, the original database no longer met all their requirements. Their solution was to create a separate database in Microsoft Excel for each new service the company required. After working with them for a couple of weeks, I assisted them in designing a new system for their unique requirements. We estimated that with the new system they would save in the range of 150 working days a year per employee, and they had three employees working the system.

This, unfortunately, is an all-too-common scenario. A lot of companies have outdated software systems that no longer fulfil all of their requirements or they have simply not identified exactly what their requirements are. When this happens, management are often afraid to spend money on updating the systems. The financial implications of creating a new system or of investing in new hardware or software may be large, but when the time savings and efficiencies are calculated companies usually find that a return on investment (ROI) will be seen in a very short space of time. In this example, the ROI was realised in less than a year, meaning that there were savings in each subsequent year.

Did you ever hear the old phrase "You must spend money to make money?" Well, exactly the same applies when it comes to time: sometimes you must spend money to save time. The advantage of spending money on enhancing productivity is that it is a totally self-financing act, as you can be guaranteed to save both time and money in a very short turnaround time.

Upgrading current systems

So how do you decide if the systems you are currently using are serving your requirements and if it is necessary to upgrade or not?

1. Does your current system or current hardware cause you any trouble or crash?
2. Are you spending money on the maintenance of your current hardware or software system?
3. Are you still using any manual systems that could be improved and made faster by upgrading to an electronic system?
4. Does it take more than thirty seconds to open an application on your computer?
5. Do network applications slow down the speed at which you would like to work?

Upgrading your computer systems can be costly and can also require downtime, which must also be taken into consideration. But in more cases that not, upgrading helps an organisation to maintain a competitive advantage through an increase in productivity and more effective business processes. Another advantage of newer systems is a reduced possibility of computer viruses attacking the system. Viruses are a risk at all times, but older software may be more vulnerable to attack than newer software.

Upgrading is not just about having the latest and fastest system and should be considered only when you are sure that the cost of not upgrading is more than the cost of upgrading! There are other options such as buying more random access memory (RAM) or buying an external hard drive for more storage; but be wary of spending money on an old system that will need to be upgraded in the near future.

When it comes to purchasing technology it is best to buy when the hardware or software that we are considering purchasing has been on the market for at least six to twelve months. This gives it time to be tried and tested by what in marketing circles would be termed the "innovators" or "early adopters". These people are the risk takers who want to try out new products on the market as soon as they are released. For example, those who purchased Windows Vista as soon as it was released will understand why waiting until something has been tried and tested is best. Windows Vista was bug-ridden and caused many problems and issues for companies and individuals.

Speed up your existing systems

There are many other ways to speed up your existing computer systems. They include the following:

Disk clean-up: Disk clean-up removes unwanted files that are on your computer. These include temporary internet files which are downloaded each time you visit the internet, downloaded program files such as ActiveX, and Java applets that are downloaded automatically when you access certain web pages. It will also remove setup log files and clean out your recycle bin if you choose for it to do so.

Disk Defragmenter: Disk fragmentation slows down your computer. Fragmentation occurs when the operating system doesn't allocate continuous space for a file. This can occur if a file has been deleted from a section of the disk, thus freeing up some space. The operating system then stores a part of a file in this free space, meaning that the file has been separated into different parts. When you go to access this file, it takes the computer longer to, first, find all the pieces of the file and then to piece them back together. Disk Defragmenter is a utility which defragments the disk and organises all the files and folders on your computer so that each occupies its own space on the disk. This speeds up reading and writing of files on the disk. According to Microsoft, Disk Defragmenter should be run monthly or when you add, remove or install new programs on the computer.

Remove unwanted programs from start-up: Many programs are set to open once windows boots up. This reduces the speed and performance of your computer. You will notice in the task bar at the bottom of your screen that there are programs that appear there when your system boots up. Programs such as Skype and printer software will automatically open up without you requesting it. These programs can be easily removed from the start-up menu. Check out the help section of your operating system to see the steps for removing these files from start-up. This will have the benefit of your computer booting up more quickly.

Remove unwanted services: Services are programs that run in the background of your computer – some are necessary; some are useless. There are many guides on the internet that will explain the function of each of the services and whether they are necessary for the smooth running of your computer. If you find that they are not required, you can see how to remove them in the help section of your operating system.

Antivirus software and spyware: Make sure your antivirus software is up to date and you scan regularly for viruses and spyware, as these can reduce the performance of your computer substantially. Unfortunately, what a lot of people notice is, once they have installed their antivirus software, their computer slows down considerably. This is not a reason to remove the software altogether – the loss of work and time needed to repair a system that has been hit by a virus will be much greater than the time lost while the antivirus software does its job. I run AVAST free with Microsoft Window's Firewall and have never had any problems. The firewalls that come with antivirus programs are usually the main culprits when it comes to reduced performance. If you have a PC I would advise you to opt for the Windows inbuilt firewall, as opposed to the ones with all the bells and whistles; you will find your system will be far quicker.

Organise your files and folders: Knowing where your files are will help you to work more quickly and prevent you wasting time searching for files or folders. Start with a good filing system, which should be regularly purged to eliminate files that are no longer in use or of value. As mentioned in Chapter 4, do not fall into the trap of storing everything on your desktop.

Increase RAM: The biggest enhancement to speed on your computer will be experienced with an upgrade of the computer's RAM. RAM is the temporary memory that a computer uses when you are busy working with your files. The more RAM your computer has, the faster it will save and process your requests.

Web-based technology

Before making any decisions about what hardware or software you are going to invest in for your company, make sure you have considered all options. For people who are on the road a lot, a natural progression is to move towards "cloud computing" or "cloud technology". This is where you pay a company for server space and all of your files are stored on the internet on a server somewhere in the sky. The beauty of this arrangement is that your files are available to you wherever the internet is. This reduces the requirement for transferring and moving files every time you leave the office. It also insures there is no duplication of files and information is accessible at all times.

Microsoft Dynamic CRM

Microsoft offers a CRM system where you need no hardware or software investment. A monthly charge allows you to access all your files, which are held on a central server, from anywhere in the world. Sales, marketing and customer service departments benefit from software that has the look and feel of Microsoft Office so won't require large investments in retraining staff. It also allows them to access customer data in the office or on the road, allowing for effective communication at all times.

Microsoft Office 365

Microsoft now gives you their familiar office package delivered from the cloud. The user can get all the functionality they are used to with Microsoft products and can access it from anywhere. Email, documents and calendars can be accessed by all employees in real time.

Google Apps for business

Google's web-based applications, messaging and collaboration apps allow businesses to have the benefits of streamlined communications without the need for high software or hardware investment. Again, as the Microsoft CRM data is stored on a central server, this offers higher security and back-up solutions. Google offers the added benefit of more storage than the industry average and allows for synching with all the popular smart phones, such as the iPhone, BlackBerry and Android.

There are many ways in which technology can speed up your existing work processes, so it is important to do the research and/or get expert advice before making an investment in hardware or software. Make sure you get a second and a third opinion before you sign on the dotted line.

Training

Recently a colleague asked me to help out one of his friends with a problem he was having with his internet connection. He was a middle manager in a large institution and had been working for the organisation for twenty years. I checked out the problem, and helped him to install his antivirus software. Then he began to ask me a few questions. At first I thought he was joking as he asked me how to create a new folder and what was the difference between "Save" and "Save as". He was not joking; he genuinely didn't know these basic features of computer usage! How could this be possible? How could someone with a senior role be doing their job effectively without these basic computer skills? Has he hidden his computer illiteracy or do his superiors know about it?

This started me thinking about how many workers do their job daily without having the skills to do it effectively. How much is this costing organisations in terms of productivity? My guess is that this could be enormous. Lack of training can lead to work being done too slowly, work being duplicated and people going about things in the wrong way because they are unaware of the shortcuts or the more efficient ways of doing things.

An untrained workplace is something we can no longer afford, especially in today's marketplace. Training must become a priority if an organisation is to continue to be productive and maintain competitiveness.

Traditionally, training has been a crucial part of most companies' yearly budgets. Organisations recognised the benefits of having a highly trained workforce. Not only does training help the individuals to complete their work more competently, it also helps to boost staff morale and motivation. Regrettably, since the global downturn, companies have had to cut their costs in many areas and the training budget was one that was severely hit or eliminated altogether. But there is a worse scenario than the company that hasn't money to invest in training, and that is the company that still has the financial resources but sees time as an issue when it comes to allowing their staff to attend training. Smart companies cannot afford to wait until the world economic mishap rights itself. They will take the lead by ensuring that all systems are functioning efficiently. Highly trained and productive workforces will be the driving forces of economic recovery.

What about ROI?

Employers are looking for return on investment and see training as yielding a long-term return. This is true of some types of training, but job-related training and personal productivity training are two types of training that should never be postponed. The results and benefits of these types of training will be evident immediately.

For example, a company with a hundred employees decides to offer 50 per cent of the staff personal workflow coaching to enhance their personal productivity. The average time saving is forty-five minutes a day. Forty-five minutes a day equals three hours and forty-five minutes a week, which adds up to almost two days a month. If we multiply this figure by fifty workers, we will see that the time the company saves is very significant. Think of the implications of savings likc that! People fail to realise the savings that can be made from productive workers. Training staff to work more efficiently will result in phenomenal gains for the organisation but can also produce workers who are more in control of their workload and better able to deal with the responsibilities that come their way.

Training helps businesses run better; it equips employees with the skills to better carry out their job-related tasks. It is important to carry out a prior assessment of training needs and requirements. Areas where there are productivity-related problems should be the areas first targeted. Levels of output should be recorded prior to doing the training and then assessed afterwards. In this way, any increase in productivity levels can be monitored and this increase can be used as proof of return on investment.

Exercise:
Identify the areas where your technology knowledge or usage could do with improvement.

Now that you have identified the areas that need attention, what is the first step you must take to make the first item on your list no longer a hindrance in your life?

8

help or hindrance?

how to guarantee the benefits

"Computers are useless – they only give us answers."

– Pablo Picasso

Technology has assisted mankind's growth and development to date and will continue to do so into the future. From spacecraft to submarines, medical equipment to toothbrushes, technological advancement has benefited us in so many ways. But the very thing that makes the world a better place can also disconnect us from who we are and what we are meant to be doing. Technology can be a thief of time and a distraction to our focus.

The changing face of work

Information technology has changed our lives as we know them. Since the early eighties and the introduction of the microcomputer into our lives and businesses, the world of work has changed drastically. From the days of collect calls home from abroad to free Skype calls on your iPhone, from endless paper pushing to processing data at the push of a button, times have definitely changed.

Technology has brought to us faster and more efficient business processes, enhanced communications, widespread sharing of information, cost efficiencies, and new and varied markets open 24/7, amongst many other benefits.

There have been so many technological additions to the world of work in the past two decades and each new technology has its shelf life. The fax has been replaced by email. Email is being succeeded by instant messaging and social media sites. In-person meetings have been bypassed by teleconferencing and videoconferencing. Our BlackBerrys, personal digital assistants (PDAs) and iPhones are becoming non-negotiable parts of who we are.

When we consider the changes that technology has brought to business in terms of efficiency and productivity, let's take a closer look at EPOS or electronic point of sale technology. EPOS technology has introduced drastic changes to the world of retail and purchasing. These systems can provide real-time information to the retailer on store traffic, sales and profitability. It can advise on shelf space allocation efficiency and shows the impact of changes in price to sales. It can inform suppliers directly of goods sold and the need for replenishment of stock. The increase in productivity that this has led to in the world of purchasing is phenomenal. The industry went from being based on a simple manual clerical system to being based on a fully computerised and integrated process.

Computerised payroll, electronic customer relationship databases, electronic mail and computerised tills were all introduced to make our lives easier and to save on the bottom line. This is great if the systems are being used as intended, correctly and efficiently. Unfortunately very often we see people going about things the wrong way. Unaware of the shortcuts and more efficient ways of doing things, they end up duplicating work and not taking advantage of the time-saving and efficient systems being used.

If one is to work productively with technology, it should only be used where it is enhancing the quality of work being done or helping to complete the work faster. Adequate software and hardware must be in place in order for workers to have the facility to work more efficiently. And, as mentioned before, employees must be trained into these systems. Clearly the amount of training required depends on the complexity of the software involved. But whatever the system, and whatever the software, ongoing training is essential for the efficient use of any system.

Social networking

The social networking explosion hit hard in the early years of the twenty-first century. In the mid-nineties, websites such as theglobe.com and sixdegrees.com came on the scene, but due to both the decline of the online advertising market and possibly being a couple of years ahead of their time, these websites didn't last. They gave way to sites such as Myspace, Friendster, Bebo, Facebook, and LinkedIn, and social networking as we know it today was born. This current phase of social networking websites allows individuals to construct a public or semi-public profile and invite friends or colleagues to connect with them online. They also allow their members to view the connections of all of their connections, creating a web or network of users online.

The scope that these websites have brought to personal and corporate global communication is phenomenal. They facilitate individuals to speak in real time to family or friends on the other side of the world, whilst also viewing their photos or playing a game. Companies can scout potential talent on websites such as LinkedIn; organisations can search for employees with relevant experience in their industry and bypass the high commission of recruitment companies. They can see online references and research the past experience of potential employees. As well as prospective employees, possible suppliers can be sourced and considered, with links to their individual websites facilitating ease of data research and collection. Employers can monitor employees' behaviour on sites such as Facebook and Twitter, so they can see whether they conduct themselves in a manner consistent with the company's reputation.

Small businesses can also benefit greatly from social networking. Making connections with other small businesses or larger organisations can assist them in getting their name and products or services known. The beauty of this method of networking or marketing is that it is predominantly free, a factor that would be very beneficial to smaller business and start-ups. LinkedIn allows you to make a connection with anyone you have done business with or friends and colleagues, allowing them to see your profile, which includes your qualifications, work history and any recommendations which you have received. There is also a facility to let your network know if you are organising any events or if you have any interesting company news to share. In Facebook, a corporate identity can also be set up in which you get friends or colleagues to "Like" your page. You can again advertise events to all your friends who "Like" your page, thus giving your message a wider reach than traditional methods of communication.

Social networking has become a worldwide phenomenon, practically overnight. As well as its obvious and many benefits, it is also fun. But it can be addictive and is definitely time consuming.

So can social networking be a help or a hindrance to our productivity?

The answer, of course, depends on what industry you work in, where your target market is and if you have been making any valuable connections and, ultimately, sales from your networking. Like most things, the data is where the proof lies, so if you have an online marketing strategy with social networking sites, it is essential to apply metrics to the time allocated to your social networking to see if the time you are investing in Facebook, LinkedIn or Twitter is actually adding value or just sucking time.

Start by monitoring your time spent on each networking site (be honest and remember to include time spent on networking sites from your phone) per week, and note down the valuable connections and possible leads that come from this time. Unfortunately networking is one of those areas that sometimes reap rewards at a much later date, but what you have to be aware of is whether the time invested is justified or not. If you are getting no new leads and just putting in hours, take a closer look at how you are spending the time allocated. Could it be put to better use? If so, change your tactics and look again at the results. If you are getting no real results, cut your losses and put your valuable time to better use elsewhere.

Remember to apply the 80/20 rule and ask yourself if what you are spending time on is the best use of your time. Remember, time is a precious limited and non-renewable resource; don't waste it browsing social networking sites and other people's lives, unless this is going to enhance your own life.

Larger monitors

Have you thought about getting a larger monitor for work? Perhaps you have been thinking about buying a second monitor. Research shows that larger monitors or dual monitors are definitely of benefit to productivity.

According to University of Utah researchers, using a larger widescreen monitor could increase productivity substantially. Tests were carried out comparing the productivity of users of an 18-inch monitor to users of a 24-inch.

They also compared using the 18-inch monitor to using two 20-inch monitors side by side. People who used two 20-inch monitors were 44 per cent more productive than the group with the single 18-inch monitor, whereas the group with the 24-inch screens was up to 52 per cent faster at completing their tasks.[5]

They deduced from the studies that multiple monitors or large widescreen configurations are recommended for use in any situation where multiple screens of information are an ordinary part of the work. A measureable increase in productivity will result and the user will find their work easier to do. Different industries and different task requirements will benefit in different ways from varying monitor set-ups, but the general research appears to show that increasing the monitor size available to you, in whichever manner, will lead to an increase in productivity.

That said, we mustn't forget to take into account the time spent on formatting, positioning and transitioning between windows, because this can be costly and non-productive. However, Professor James Anderson, who led the above study, would agree with the opinion that once you go multi-screen you will never go back. He himself works with a three-screen display.

Some of the many benefits of a multi-screen system are:

1. Being able to look at notes on one screen while typing or working on the other screen

2. Comparing drafts of documents

3. Comparing images

4. Being able to see all columns of a spreadsheet

---

[5] J.A. Anderson, "Productivity, Screens and Aspect Ratios: A Comparison of Single, Traditional Aspect, Dual Traditional Aspect, and Single Widescreen Aspect Computer Displays Over Simulated Office Tasks across Performance and Usability", CIC Report 200719, Salt Lake City, UT: CIC, 2007.

5. Having different programs open and in view at the same time

Benefits of larger screens in general:

1. Ease of copying and pasting from one document to another
2. Being able to see all palettes in programs such as Photoshop
3. Being able to see both design and development views in programs such as Dreamweaver
4. Reduction in scrolling time

The best advice I can give is to try out somebody else's configuration before you invest in a new monitor or monitors. Each individual's requirement should be taken into account, and assessed as to whether there is a requirement for a dual-screen system or just a larger monitor. Companies like Google and Microsoft are full of dual screens, as are many of the banks and larger organisations. Again, it is wise to be careful before spending, as many workers find their productivity falling when they have two screens open, as they often keep their email open on one of the screens and fall into the trap of reacting to incoming email and allowing themselves to be distracted from the work they should be occupied with.

Productivity software/apps

Most of us in our life time have used productivity software without even knowing it. Productivity software includes the programs that we use daily, such as spreadsheet programs, word processing, presentation software, etc. These programs allow us to get our work done efficiently. What makes these programs more productive is if they can pre-empt what the user wants and deliver it to them, allowing the user to work as quickly and effectively as possible. Microsoft Office is one of the most popular productivity software suites, perhaps because it successfully anticipates the user's requirements, or maybe because Microsoft's software dominates the market for other reasons. What we do know is that it allows us to get a lot of our work done in much less time than if we were to do it manually.

One of the benefits of using intuitive software is that it doesn't delay the user in any way in completing their tasks. The user gets accustomed to where the features are, and the more familiar they are with the functions the faster they can complete their work – that is until some developer somewhere decides that it would be more user-friendly to display all the menu options on the page under new headings, instead of nicely tucked away under the headings that we are all familiar with.

Other than the Office programs that we use daily there are many other programs that one can use to become more productive and get things done more quickly. But are they necessary, and does their implementation add more layers of complexity to our productivity or does it help to simplify things?

Task management

There are a lot of task management apps and to-do list software out there, and I have tried out quite a few. One of my favourites is Remember The Milk (RTM) (www.rememberthemilk.com). Maybe it's the quirky name or the simplicity of use, but RTM is definitely one of the best. It allows you to create to-do lists for today, tomorrow and this week, while also being able to assign a task to a category such as work, home, a particular project, etc. Another advantage of RTM is that your account is set up online so that all of your tasks are visible from your online account, just in case your phone loses battery, which is not so much a problem if you are a BlackBerry or Android user. RTM is compatible with iPhone, BlackBerry, Android and Google apps, to name but a few.

There are many other popular and effective task management apps, including:

• Todoodle: www.toodledo.com
• Zenbe Lists: www.zenbe.com/lists

All of these programs, and many more, have more or less the same function. To decide which one is best for you, you will have to consider the platform you are using, the degree of detail you like to work with and whether simplicity or complexity is synonymous with your work style. In saying this I would recommend you take a look at some productivity blogs or technology review sites to get some ideas on what they are all about. At the end of the day, remember that what you are aiming for is simplicity and getting things done faster and more efficiently, so don't spend too long deciding. Usually the simpler the better!

Getting Things Done®

Official software coming from the David Allen camp is the Getting Things Done® for Outlook® add-in, which allows you to customise your Outlook to implement the GTD method.   eProductivity for IBM Lotus Notes® is another add-in that brings the power of GTD to Lotus Notes. Both of these programs will allow you to follow the GTD method and organise your life and work using Outlook.

There appear to be many pieces of software that, while not officially endorsed by the David Allen group, have been developed to tie in with the GTD methodology. So, if you are a GTD fan, check out some of the following websites:

- My Life Organized: www.mylifeorganized.net
- Nozbe: www.nozbe.com/gtd/index
- Viira (GTD with BlackBerry): www.kartamobile.com
- Omnifocus: www.omnigroup.com/products/omnifocus

Text replacement software

Text replacement software allows you to insert pieces of text into a document or email. This reduces time spent re-typing repetitive words and phrases such as "Please don't hesitate to contact me if you have any further questions" or your web address or email address. ShortKeys is a very powerful program that allows you to do all this and more. It is not free but it can save you a significant amount of time daily if you type a lot of documents on your computer.

Mind mapping software

Mind mapping software is used to create links between concepts or ideas. It is generally used for idea creation or by students for studying. There are many pieces of software on the market, one of the most popular ones being MindMap by Tony Buzan: www.thinkbuzan.com/intl/home.

Other available software can be found at the following websites.

- www.mindgenius.com
- www.mindjet.com

For free open source mind-mapping software, go to www. xmind.net.

Note taking

Another very useful piece of software is Evernote (www. evernote.com/about/home.php). Evernote allows you to capture anything from a thought to a piece of text to a photo. Once captured, you can organise these notes and store them, making them easily accessible. It is very useful for planning trips or projects as it allows you to store ideas and anything else you may want to keep in the same place to make it accessible.

Voice recognition software

Voice recognition software can be a great boost to many industries such as the legal profession or anyone who attends lots of meetings or interviews people for a living. This software allows you to transcript information without the tedious typing that is usually necessary.

Typing tutor

Yes, by learning how to type with all ten fingers, not two or four or eight, you can increase your productivity enormously. Imagine being able to write ten times faster than you can now? Mavis Beacon is always a winner (www.mavisbeacon.com), but if you want a free tutor without all the frills, go for www.typefastertypingtutor.com.

The above are all fantastic task management tools, and all do great things to move us forwards, onwards and upwards. My advice would be, if you are going to work with a task management tool, to chose just one and try to keep it simple. These programs can absorb some of the time that they are designed to save. Text replacement software is definitely a wise move as it saves time and involves very little in terms of setting it up. Mind mapping tools are essential as study tools or for preparing presentations, and they can be very useful for certain projects. But there were also instances, in my experience, when the time invested in them didn't see a reward. However, if you are a very visual person, a mind-mapping program would be a great addition to your productivity tool box.

If you are feeling confused or overwhelmed by all the possibilities, the best thing to do is to buy yourself a lovely leather notebook and keep everything in it. For some, paper will always be king. The most important thing is that nothing gets forgotten or left behind, and if you can achieve this with a paper-based system then full speed ahead.

9

managing email overload

be master of your inbox

"I get mail, therefore I am."

– Scott Adams

Email programs have now become a crucial component of every computer installation, as constant connectivity becomes more and more important for today's knowledge worker. According to a *Wall Street Journal* report of 27 November 2007, the amount of time in the work day spent processing emails had increased from 17 per cent in 2003 to 23 per cent in 2006, and at the time was estimated to have increased to 41 per cent by 2009.

So has something gone wrong? Does this email explosion have any benefits for us? Or is it just sapping our time and disturbing our focus from the things that add value to our working day?

Email has become our main link to the external world; it is the fastest and most direct mode of communication that business has ever known. We can link to large audiences worldwide for free.

We are all aware that email is a tool that has transformed business communications in the past couple of decades, but learning to use it efficiently is paramount in order to experience its full impact and advantages in the world of work.

Training is an essential issue when it comes to coping with the email explosion. It is assumed that everyone can send and receive an email, but there is a lot more to our email programs that can influence how effective or how disorganised we become.

The invention of email is a blessing for most organisations, but the flipside of this is email overload – part of the information overload phenomenon.

Take the following scenario: You go into work at 9.00 a.m. You make a cup of coffee. You say hello to your colleagues. When you sit down at your desk ready to work it's already 9.30 a.m. You have a very important report to write but before you begin you decide to check your email in case there is anything important to be dealt with (something more important than the urgent report!). There are a couple of personal mails, which you answer, and then a few questions from colleagues that need to be addressed, so you do that too. It is now 10.15 a.m. You go to the bathroom and meet one of the department's managers in the hallway who asks you to come to his office so you can answer a few questions for him on the project you are working on. You get back to your desk at 11.00 a.m. At coffee break, you have another cup of coffee and come back and check your email before you settle down to writing the report. Your phone rings and you have a short conversation. You spend fifteen minutes writing the report. Then you get an email notification so you check your mail again and see there's an email from your boss, which has to be answered straight away. He is looking for feedback on a meeting you attended with a big supplier. You need to check up on something before you reply so you go onto the internet to check out the supplier's website. While you are online, you remember you have to buy flights to London for the trade show next month so you take a quick look at flights and then go back to answering your boss's email. It is now lunch time...Need I go on? Does this sound familiar?

Email has made us believe that multitasking is a normal part of our day, but the truth is that multitasking doesn't work. Many people believe that multitasking is the only way they can cope in our world of task and information overload, but the reality is that the brain is incapable of actually focusing on two things at the same time. A frontal part of the brain called Broadman's Area 10 is responsible for the brain switching from task to task, and while we may think we are multitasking we are actually getting good at switching from task to task more seamlessly.

But switching tasks loses you time and focus. Unfortunately most modern offices are set up in a manner that you are expected to be able to work, answer questions from passers by and not get distracted by conversations that are happening all around you – and of course respond to every email sent to you at all times of the day. All of this equals productivity disaster.

Company culture plays a big part in whether it is easy for workers to be productive or not. It is vital that the company's leadership understands the pitfalls of the open plan office and the productivity nightmare caused by constant monitoring of email. When the correct culture is established and the leadership of the company realise that emails should be checked only at certain times during the day, the training must follow.

Most employees are not given training in email usage. Very few people know how to process and organise their emails. Not enough companies have email usage policies and fewer still communicate their company's email culture to all employees. The result? Email inboxes that have thousands of emails sitting there cluttering up your electronic space. How many of those thousands of emails have still got tasks that need to be completed? How many of those emails can be deleted and how many need to be filed for reference? The statistics show that, on average, 50 per cent of our mail can be deleted, and the other 50 per cent is either information we want to keep for reference or items that need to be scheduled for later.

What are the advantages of a clear inbox? Many clients begin a personal productivity session with no intention of deleting any of the emails in their inbox but just want a way to ensure that all the emails are dealt with in a timely manner. They don't see the benefits of a clear inbox; they don't realise that if you have a couple of thousand or even a couple of hundred emails in your inbox it is possible that you have overlooked some of the tasks that need to be completed. Very often something will fall through the net and not get done, but worse than this is the uncertainty that you are carrying around when you are constantly unsure of whether you have your finger on the pulse or if you have missed something. Emails in your inbox are cluttering your work environment. How many times do you glance back over the inbox to see if there is anything else to be dealt with? By keeping your inbox clear of emails at a minimum you will not only feel more in control, you will speed up your response time and reduce your stress and workload.

Managing email overload should begin with the following areas:

- Incoming messages
- Reducing time writing and responding to emails
- Organising and prioritising
- Email processing
- Company culture

Incoming messages

The first action to take is to reduce the number of incoming messages. Analyse the source and ask yourself the following questions:

- Is the email work related? If you are receiving personal emails to your work address, advise your friends or family to send their emails to a personal email address that you check only when you have free time to do so. If a friend or family member needs to contact you during work hours, ask them to phone you or send you a text message. If you don't have a personal email address, set one up. Always give out the personal address when shopping online or when filling in forms, etc.

- If you are receiving newsletters, are they adding value to your work life? If not, unsubscribe or use a different email address to receive newsletters.

- Are you receiving RSS[6] feeds? Again, try and limit the number you are receiving to the ones that are beneficial to your job, or subscribe under a different email address.

- Do you subscribe to a number of mailing lists? Take a look at all the company or customer mailing lists that you are a member of and decide if you can take your name off any of these.

- Do you receive a lot of spam? One way to avoid spam is to never display your email address on your website as it will be picked up to be used by a spammer. There are a few methods you can use to avoid displaying your address. One is to write your email address in the following format (ciara(at)ciaraconlon(dot)com), but this may be confusing for some inexperienced web users. Many websites use contact forms but these forms can be unpopular so an alternative to this is to post your email address as an image so that spam

---

[6] RSS stands for really simple syndication and allows you to receive website or blog content directly to your inbox.

crawlers cannot read the address. If you are a member of a forum or any other online community, don't post your work email address; use your personal one. If spam continues to be a problem, talk to your email service provider and ask them to set your spam filter to high. If this still doesn't solve the problem, there are programs you can install so that all emails have to be verified by the sender before they are allowed into your inbox.

- Use the phone. Do you remember that form of communication that we used before email? If you want to ask a colleague a question, don't email them. Just pick up the phone and ask the question. If you want to reduce the number of emails you receive, you should reduce the number of emails that you send.

Reducing time writing and responding

We can then try to reduce the time spent on writing and responding to emails:

- If you are sending an email asking somebody to do something for you, thank them in advance so that you don't have to send an email afterwards saying thank you. Please, please don't waste bandwidth sending emails to say you're welcome. If you don't feel comfortable thanking in advance, wait until you send your next email to the person and thank them then.

- When you send an email that doesn't require a response, write "No response necessary".

- If you want to send a short informative message, write it in the subject field. For example, "Meeting cancelled [EOM]." By including [EOM], which means end of message, the recipient doesn't have to click on and open the email, which will save them time.

- Try to ask only one or two questions per email, and definitely avoid having more than one topic per email. Even though we are trying to reduce the number of emails in our inbox, it is much faster and efficient to process one topic at a time and deal with the email once rather than having to keep coming back to the same email to check that all items are dealt with.

- If you receive an email telling you that you will receive money or free goods for sending the email on to ten or twenty people in your inbox – this is a hoax. Neither will a company donate money to charity depending on the number of emails you send to your address book – that, too, is a hoax. Unfortunately in this world we rarely get something for nothing, especially not over email.

- Use a text replacement program. Programs that replace a key stroke with predefined text, for example, ShortKeys Lite (www.shortkeyslite.com), can be invaluable. Let's say you always end your emails with the following chunk of text: "Please don't hesitate to contact me if you have any further questions". Imagine if you could type a predefined character on the keyboard and the text would be automatically inserted into your email or document. You can use this tool for your website or email signature or anything else that you repetitively type; it can all be inserted in just a keystroke.

- It never ceases to amaze me how many people don't use an email signature. If I were to type my signature every time I write an email, and let's say I write a conservative twenty emails a day, five days a week, and it takes me fifteen seconds to type my signature (kind regards – my name – my phone number), this adds up to twenty-five minutes a week. What a waste of time! It will take you maximum five minutes to set up an email signature Go to your email program's help menu to find out how to set up a signature.

Organising and prioritising

Organising the way you receive your email can reduce the number of emails in your inbox and allow you to see and deal with the important emails first.

In Microsoft Outlook, a rule is a set of conditions, actions and exceptions that processes and organises messages automatically and that is triggered by an event. A rule tells your email program what should be done with a particular email once received. Rules are the answer to the prayers of those people with overloaded inboxes. They are powerful and flexible and you can set up as many as you like.

There are a myriad of reasons to set up a rule. Here are just a few examples:

- You receive lots of emails where you are in the Cc or Bcc line. This usually means that these emails are not as important for you as an email where you are in the "To" field. You can set up a rule to move these emails automatically into a folder called "Cc mails" that you can browse at a later stage. You can put exceptions on these rules, for example, unless a certain project name is mentioned or unless the email is from your managing director.

- You receive emails with FYI (for your information) in the subject line. This generally means that the email is not so important. A folder could be set up for these mails also.

- If you receive emails from a certain distribution list regarding a particular project, you can have these automatically placed in a folder set up for this particular project.

- You can set up a sound alert when an email arrives from your managing director. You may want to check this email immediately.

These are only a few samples; there are hundreds of different combinations that may be suitable for your work environment and workload. Don't overlook this powerful tool – it may take you a couple of minutes to set up each rule but the time savings in the long term are huge.

Some people don't like to move emails to different folders and prefer to keep all emails that still have to be acted on in the inbox. One way to do this is by using categories. Categories can be assigned to different types of emails. So, for example, you can put all family emails into the family category and all accounts emails into the accounts category. You could have a category for your friends, email newsletters, your team, your boss, your clients and your important projects. To automatically assign a category to an email, you set up a rule: list the relevant people and key words so that if an email arrives from these people or with these words in it, it is assigned to a particular category. This rule can take some time to set up, especially if you want to have categories for all emails received, but it can be a very good way to decide which emails are important and need to be processed first.

Lotus Notes also uses the rules function. However, other email programs have alternative methods to organise the emails received, such as filters in Mozilla Thunderbird.

Email processing

First and foremost, before we go any further, turn off all email notifications – no bells, no envelopes, no dings! Emails should only be processed at assigned times during the day. You must be in control of your inbox. Don't allow your inbox to become your to-do list.

The secret to successful email processing is "batching", i.e. setting times in the day to check and respond to emails. But processing emails doesn't just mean replying to the emails in your inbox, because, as you know, there may be ten emails in your inbox but they may contain large amounts of work that need to be done. Processing means taking an email and deciding what you are going to do with it. Is there work in the email that needs to be scheduled or is just a quick response required? Maybe it's an email just for your information. If so, can it be filed immediately?

If you ever want to be one of those people who have zero or very few emails in their inbox, you must create the new habit of dealing with each email one at a time. If you have a system in place to process your email, you can gain more control, improve your response time and keep up with your workload.

A useful system to process your inbox is that of organisational expert Barbara Hemphill – the FAT system (file, act or trash). An alternative is the four Ds of decision making: delete it, do it, delegate it or defer it.

Before you can process your email effectively, you must set up an efficient filing or reference system in your email program. This can be done by creating folders for files that need to be kept. It is very important to make the classification early on that reference items are not items that need to be acted on. A file or document is only filed when it has been acted on; it is information you keep in case you need to access it at a later date. Your reference system can be added to as you start to process your email and see what folders are needed.

Start processing email by quickly scanning your email for important or urgent emails. You can filter according to the person who sent you the email. Quickly scan the emails in your reading pane to see how important they are. You can do the initial filtering by subject or by date sent.

Then take the first email and deal with it before moving on to the next email. You must take control and make a decision on what needs to be done with the email before moving on. Do not fall into the trap of "Not sure what to do about this one. I will come back to it." If you do this, you will have taken the first step on the way to email overload.

Remember to use the following rules when processing your email:

1. If you have no need for the email, delete it.
2. If you wish to hold onto it for reference, create a reference folder section in your personal email folders.
3. If the email requires action, make a decision on what needs to be done.

If you can respond to the email in less than two minutes, do so straight away and then delete or file the email. If you need more time to respond, plan the work that needs doing by putting it in your calendar or your to-do or task list.

Each time you process your email, be it daily, twice a day or three times a day, you must follow the FAT rule – file, act or trash. Never move onto the next item until you have made a decision about what to do with the email.

Research shows that 50 per cent of your email can be deleted, 30 per cent can be delegated or completed in less than two minutes, and 20 per cent can be deferred to your calendar or task list. So if you follow the FAT rule, you can have the respectable clutter-free inbox you've only dreamed of!

Company culture

Instilling a company culture for effective email usage is an important step on the road to clear and organised inboxes. There are many ways in which you can do this.

- Have a company email usage policy document, stating how email is to be used and advising employees of methods to reduce quantities of emails sent, etc.

- Have a company intranet. This allows for employees to access information easily and not to have to ask so many questions over email. If company information is easily accessible, this should reduce the need for unnecessary internal communication.

- Send fewer emails to receive fewer emails.

- Use the phone. Encourage people to ask you their questions over the phone.

- Suggest email-free days. Many companies use Friday as their internal email-free day. This shows people that they can actually live without internal email and that sometimes issues can be solved more quickly by picking up the phone or by walking to the person's desk.

- Don't Cc or Bcc unless necessary. Very often, copies of emails are sent to CYA (cover your ass) or ensure that everyone is kept informed of certain happenings in the company. Find out if the person you are copying in on the email really needs all the details or if they just need to know that the report or the quotation was sent.

- Establish a culture of not sending "ASAP" emails, i.e. emails that ask for work to be done as soon as possible. Be specific. Give a reasonable and time specific deadline. If you are the receiver of an ASAP email, respond by giving a time and date that you will have the work completed by. If this is not acceptable to the sender, they will reply and tell you so.

Productivity tips from Section 4 – Technology

1. Ensure that your hardware is not slowing down your systems.

2. Ensure that your software is contributing to an efficient workflow.

3. Consider training to enhance skills and knowledge of systems.

4. Don't fall prey to the distractions of the internet and social networking.

5. Invest in a larger monitor or dual-screen system.

6. Reduce incoming mail (e.g. unsubscribe to unnecessary newsletters).

7. Reduce time spent writing and replying to emails.

8. Implement a company protocol for electronic communications.

section 5 – leadership and productivity

10

leadership

the productive leader

"A leader leads by example, whether he intends to or not."

– Author unknown

Leaders come in different shapes and sizes and can be found in many realms of life. Presidents, priests, coaches, teachers – their jobs are diverse but they share an objective to motivate and inspire. But what determines the quality of leadership? Down through the ages philosophers and psychologists alike have pondered over what makes a good leader. Theories on what makes a leader date back to the time of Plato and Aristotle. Some would describe leadership as an art, but is it an art that can be learnt or is it a talent we are born with?

The trait theorists[7] were of the view that the characteristics required for an individual to become an effective leader were innate and could not be learnt. Therefore, leadership traits

---

[7] "Leadership trait theory assumes there are distinctive physical and psychological characteristics accounting for leadership effectiveness." From Adrian Furnham, *The Psychology of Behaviour at Work,* UK: Psychology Press, 1997, p. 518. Trait theory was prevalent in the 1930s and 1940s. The theory is no longer seen as reputable. However, in recent years, some skills identified by the theory are now seen as valid.

could be identified and people who possessed these characteristics and leadership potential could be recognised. Many psychometric tests and interviews were carried out to try and ascertain the traits that were essential to make a leader, but the results were unclear and non-replicable. The list of traits seemed to grow and grow, leading to confusion and disputes. It was also noted that people who possessed the leadership traits weren't always leaders.

After the second world war theorists moved towards the behavioural approach to leadership. They argued that the actions of leaders, rather than what their personal traits or abilities were, were more likely to help us determine what makes a leader. There have been many other theories of leadership through the years and, as with all historical psychology studies, some theories will continue to be held in high regard whilst others will be discredited as time passes, but all have contributed something to modern thinking on leadership. However, many of these theories omit to mention the essential part that influence plays in leadership.

Modern theories of leadership

What is influence? Influence is the ability to affect the perceptions, attitudes or behaviour of others. The two contemporary approaches to leadership thinking both emphasise the importance of the role influence plays in leadership. One of these theories is that of charismatic leadership, which defines leadership as the charisma to motivate and inspire. The charismatic concept dates back to ancient Greece, but the modern thinking is attributed to the work of Robert J. House.[8] The followers of the charismatic leader

---

[8] Robert J. House is a management expert who first proposed the theory of charismatic leadership in 1977, based on research findings from a variety of social science disciplines. He has a PhD in Management from Ohio State University.

identify with the leader and the mission of the leader; they usually exhibit great loyalty for and confidence in the leader. It was later suggested that charismatic leadership was just one of the components of a broader theory – that of trans-formational leadership, whereby the leader shifts the values, beliefs and needs of their followers. A transformational leader recognises the need for change, creates a vision to guide the change, translates this vision into organisational goals and communicates these goals clearly to his subordi-nates, all the time inspiring them to achieve.

Modern leadership experts all advocate the idea of personal leadership combined with leading others. They would agree with Gandhi when he said "Be the change you want to see in the world", or, in other words, lead by example. It is therefore essential for someone in a leadership position to be highly self-aware, and to recognise and understand his or her own emotions and personality. Being self-aware allows a person to recognise their strengths and work on their weaknesses.

Behaviours of a leader

Personal productivity

A leader should display all the behaviours they want their team to exhibit. If they want their team to work more effi-ciently and productively, it would be in their interest to work productively, setting the example of working in an efficient, methodical way. The leader must be in control of their own work, and be focused and stress free. They can achieve this by having an efficient workflow system to help them stay in control of their workload and work environment. A leader should be able to plan and schedule, keep their appointments and stay focused on the priorities without getting stressed by the impending tasks that need to be completed. This personal productivity and efficiency will give an excellent example to their employees and help to foster good habits in the work-place. If an employee is more in control of their workload, they will suffer less stress and be happier at work.

Another part of being personally productive is the importance of being a good delegator. It is essential for a leader not to do any work that someone else could do for them. A leader needs to have time to lead, and they can do this by delegating effectively to their team. Thus, not only does the leader free up their own time for strategic thinking and creativity, they also display confidence in their employee's abilities, helping to motivate the employees further.

Communication and interpersonal skills

The way a manager interacts with people is just as important as being a good example. In Biblical terms: "Do unto others as you would have them done unto you." People notice how you treat them; they notice when you are impatient, annoyed, irritated or frustrated. Therefore, recognising and preventing the behaviours that may upset and irritate others is necessary for the efficient running of any team or group.

It is important that a manager is not only self-aware and in control of their own personal actions, but that they also have highly developed interpersonal skills. A leader's role is to motivate others, and in order to do this they must be trusted and instil confidence in their team. Interpersonal skills include having excellent communication skills, being able to interact with people and empathy. If a leader does not have strong interpersonal skills, they probably won't earn the respect they need and deserve to lead a team successfully.

In his book *The Seven Habits of Highly Successful People*, Stephen Covey speaks about a concept that he considers very useful in dealing with people – the win/win agreement. Covey explains that a win/win situation is one where you seek mutual benefit in all human interactions. Human beings should not seek to win to the detriment of another; one should always seek to reach an agreement or a solution which is mutually beneficial to both parties. Both parties should always feel good about the decision and feel committed to the action plan decided on. This is a very important concept when dealing with teams. In many traditional leadership scenarios the leader took on the authoritarian style of leadership or, as some would describe it, "My way or the highway". Leaders did not see the need or probably the advantage of taking into account the opinions and requirements of their team members. Decisions were made by the leader for the good of the organisation. This style of leadership does not foster loyalty or commitment. Employees do not feel motivated or allied to the team or the organisation, and, without the motivation and cooperation of employees, productivity suffers.

In all team scenarios the spirit of cooperation, as opposed to competition, should be fostered at all costs. This is a principle based on a belief that it is always possible for both sides to gain. Leaders are dependent on followers for support; team members and group members may also have expertise that a leader may need. Leaders must also recognise their strengths and their dependence on their team as a result, and the great advantages that can be gained from building positive relationships that are mutually beneficial.

Ability to motivate

In order to have motivated employees, they must be inspired by both the vision of the organisation and by its leader. If the leader is a good communicator and is emphatic towards the employees there is a good likelihood that the employees will respect the leader and the leader's vision, and will therefore work efficiently towards achieving the organisation's goals.

Flexibility

Flexibility can assist in motivating employees. Good employers are sensitive to their employees' needs. Good employees have a healthy balance between work and life. By recognising and allowing for the fact that your employees are whole people, with responsibilities and commitments outside of work, you will inevitably gain their respect and commitment. Flexible employers equal happy employees. Be open to the possibility of doing things differently. It is not always necessary to stick rigidly to the nine-to-five Monday-to-Friday schedule to get the job done right.

Recognition

Human beings thrive on recognition. If somebody does a good job, make sure you let them know. Studies in the US have shown how saying "Thank you" and "Well done" to employees can have a favourable effect on productivity. If you let somebody know that you are happy with their work, you are likely to receive the same quality of work, if not better, in the future. Praise where praise is due.

Health and fitness

When asked in an interview about his best productivity tip, Richard Branson replied, "Workout". The fitter your employees are, the better they will perform. Therefore it is wise to encourage a fitness policy at work. Fit people suffer less stress. Fit people have more energy and generally have a more positive outlook on life.

Empathy

Another skill which a leader should practise is that of empathy. Empathy is the ability to understand another person's thoughts and feelings. An empathetic leader is an effective leader. By understanding those around you, you are in an advantaged position when it comes to communicating with these people. Covey's Habit 5 is "Seek first to understand then to be understood."

Empathy is closely linked to having good listening skills. Listening is a skill that all should nurture. Very few people in this world are truly good listeners. We listen to the parts of conversations that we are interested in. We filter out the uninteresting parts and zone in on the parts that we relate to. A lot of the time we are just waiting to contribute our bit to the conversation because, of course, what we have to say is a lot more stimulating and accurate than what everybody else is saying. In truth, most of us are bad listeners. A good leader has to be a good listener. They have to know and understand their team in order to get the most out of them. They have to first understand their team before they can hope to get the team to understand them and their objectives.

Empathy is a concept leadership expert Robin Sharma deals with in his book *Leadership Wisdom by the Monk Who Sold His Ferrari*. Sharma advocates the concept "Manage by mind, lead by heart". People are emotional and irrational beings. Therefore to lead them we must lead with our emotions, empathy and understanding. That said, we must not forget about the ability to influence and the existence of power that is necessary in the position – not power in the autocratic sense but that which results from managerial competency and technical expertise. Charisma can also be a source of control, as charismatic leaders have a commanding presence that can assist in influencing behaviour. It is important for others to be aware of a leader's power and his or her powers of persuasion.

This supposition would tie in with the author of *Emotional Intelligence* Daniel Goleman's thinking that the only consistency when it comes to identifying the traits of effective leaders is that they all have a high degree of emotional intelligence.

Emotional intelligence

Goleman says that the most effective leaders have a high level of emotional intelligence, or EQ as he calls it. He believes that the traditional intelligence quotient (IQ) and technical skills are not irrelevant, but that these are the entry level requirements for executive positions. Goleman did a large amount of research with trained psychologists and attempted to develop a competency model to help organisations identify and train leaders. When he analysed the data from his research he found what was expected – that intellect was a driver of outstanding performance. Cognitive skills, such as big-picture thinking and long-term vision, were particularly important. But when he calculated the ratio of technical skills to IQ to EQ as the ingredients of excellent performance, EQ was twice as important as the other two for jobs at all levels and the most important for jobs at the highest levels.

In a study carried out by David McClelland on a global food and beverage company in 1996, he found that when senior managers had a critical mass of EQ capabilities, their divisions outperformed yearly goals by 20 per cent.

So what is emotional intelligence? Goleman says that EQ is born largely in the neurotransmitters of the brain's limbic system, which is the area that governs feelings, impulses and drives. EQ consists of the following five components: self-awareness, self-regulation, motivation, empathy and social skills.

Self-awareness is the ability to recognise and understand your own moods and emotions and their effect on others. The traits associated with self-awareness are self-confidence and realistic self-assessment. People who have a high degree of self-awareness are usually not overly critical and tend to be both honest and realistic. Being self-aware helps a person to recognise their weaknesses and accept openly constructive criticism. This is a quality that is essential for good leadership. A leader must assess critically and objectively their personal capabilities as well as those of their team or organisation, and then must make informed decisions on the basis of this judgement.

Self-regulation is the ability to control or redirect disruptive impulses and moods – in other words, to think before acting. People naturally have biological impulses that drive our emotions. We cannot do away with these impulses but we can try to control and manage them. A leader must regulate their reactions and take time to choose their reaction to a specific event. A leader who is reasonable will create an environment of trust and fairness. A lot of the negative things that happen in organisations are down to a lack of self-regulation. Self-regulated individuals are usually more open to change. They will not react negatively to change; they will try to take time to think about the reasons for and benefits of the change.

Motivation is the trait that all effective leaders possess. They are driven to achieve far beyond their own and everybody else's expectations. Many people are driven to achieve, but they are driven by external factors – money, reward, recognition. But effective leaders are motivated by a deep desire to achieve for the sake of achievement. Such people seek out creative challenges and love to learn; they are always eager to explore new approaches and pursue new challenges.

Empathy is the most easily recognisable trait; it is easy to identify a person who considers the feelings of others. Empathy is the ability to understand the emotional make-up of another person. It is an essential trait when dealing with and working with people. Empathetic leaders in organisations thoughtfully consider employees' feelings along with other factors in the process of making intelligent decisions.

Possessing social skills is the ability to manage relationships with others. In doing so, it is important to find common ground and build rapport with people, which are vital components in building and leading teams. Social skills are the culmination of other aspects of EQ. People who tend to be effective at managing relationships are likely to be good at managing their own emotions and are generally empathetic towards the feelings of others.

We can see from Goleman's research that the attributes of EQ are not just desirable components of being a good leader, but, along with intelligence and technical abilities, are fundamental to the role.

Leadership is about being the best you can be at any given time, in all areas of your life. The productive leader needs to create a shared strategic vision for their organisation. Being a good leader means vocalising this vision and ensuring the team are committed and sufficiently motivated to achieve the vision.

An effective leader must be personally productive and well organised to get things done, but the further advantages of being productive, the enhanced focus, the clarity in vision, the relaxed calm are all highly sought after attributes and somewhat essential to leading successfully.

On the opposing side, what can happen if a leader is unproductive and doesn't inspire confidence or motivation in his subordinates? What are the potential negative effects of a leader who is not liked, who perhaps micromanages or is so stressed out that they create an environment of tension and stress?

The effects are probably greater and much more serious than one might imagine. Consider the case of the micromanager. They spend their day checking up on all members of their team, rewriting reports, changing priorities, updating procedures and ultimately disrupting the flow of work the team may have initiated. The manager loses time for their own creative or strategic thinking because they are so busy thinking for other people. Their own work suffers as a result and they will usually suffer from stress because of the enormity of the range of tasks they must do, or think they must do. But the worst part of this is that it is not just the manager's productivity that suffers – all the team members will be affected by his behaviour too. Any attempt at creative thinking or thinking outside the box will usually not be accepted by the micromanager as it may create something that they are not in control of. The team members will be frustrated and irritated most of the time and sometimes a build-up of these feelings will lead to anger. They will eventually feel unappreciated and de-motivated as their contributions are not valued. This lack of motivation will have direct implications for the employees' productivity levels. Unhappy and unmotivated employees will generally not give the best customer service in the world, so the company's relationship with its customers will also suffer. Ultimately, this micromanager will have a huge negative impact on the company's revenue stream.

What about the average middle manager who is not as organised as they should be, who spends long hours trying to get everything done, who takes work home, and feels stressed and overwhelmed by work a lot of the time? Most organisations have at least one of these managers, and more still have a multitude of them. This manager is your average hard worker. He or she works as many hours as are necessary to get the job done.

People who are stressed and overwhelmed by work have a tendency to forget about priorities, not reply to emails, forget to return phone calls, and so on. Customer relations can be affected. Time is wasted by superiors checking up on and discussing problems that may have arisen due to the ball being dropped at some stage or other. Subordinates are not as organised and clear about their work and priorities. Although this type of middle manager may be highly skilled and appear to be effective a good percentage of the time, they also incur costs for the organisation, through loss of productivity – their own and their team's – and loss of their superiors' time.

What such managers don't realise is that they can be much more efficient in how they go about planning and doing their work. By prioritising more effectively and eliminating unnecessary work, they can knock hours off their working week, reduce their stress levels, and motivate and inspire those around them on a daily basis. If they fail to do this, their work along with their team's work will suffer. They could gain hours daily for more creative and strategic thinking. They could be a powerful role model for their team and inspire all around them to be more efficient.

Productivity and leadership go hand in hand. Competent, efficient leaders spell good results, and not only is this reflected in their personal standard of work, it shows in the work of those around them. Leaders must lead by example in all facets of their work life. Workers must work harder, be more productive, and get better results. Real leaders walk their talk; they show their people how to get the results they want to see. They communicate with their people and work towards bringing out the best in those around them. The productive leader inspires, motivates and ultimately gets things done.

Productivity tips from Section 5 – Leadership and Productivity

1. Lead by example to encourage efficiency.

2. Be flexible and open to new ways of doing things.

3. Encourage health and fitness; healthy people are happier and more motivated.

4. Practise empathy; it will help to instil confidence and inspire loyalty.

5. Monitor managers to ensure their practices are not having a detrimental effect on the productivity of those around them.

section 6 – positivity

11

the power of positivity

how optimism and positivity can help get things done

"For myself I am an optimist – it does not
seem to be much use being anything else."

– Winston Churchill

How can optimism, positivity and happiness affect our ability to get things done and achieve our goals?

As some of you may be aware, I write a blog at www.ciara-conlon.com. My blog came about because I wanted to write about productivity, and I wanted to debate the benefits of focus and goal setting and suggest solutions to the problems of disorganisation and procrastination. I knew before I started that people needed help organising themselves, because when I told people what I did for a living, a large percentage told me they would benefit from my services. I found from writing my blog and seeing the comments from others that, even though people had a need for organisation and increased efficiency, what they wanted was positivity. On the days I wrote about positivity and optimism, I would get the most reaction or interaction on my sites. So my productivity site turned into a productivity and positivity site. Give the people what they want, the marketers say. If the people want positivity then I decided I should give it to them.

I decided to study positive psychology and optimism. I wanted to find out what the benefits of optimism were, other than the obvious.

Could optimism help us to achieve more in life? I had heard previously that optimists tend to be more successful in life; they are healthier and earn more money; and of course they are happier. But why is that so?

The next question I wanted an answer to was whether optimism was an innate characteristic or whether it could be learned. What I discovered was that, not only are we a naturally optimistic race, but that positivity and optimism can assist us in most areas of life.

The optimism bias

It may be hard to believe under the current political and economic circumstances but scientists say that, as a race, we are more optimistic than realistic. We tend to look on the bright side of life; we hugely underestimate our chances of getting divorced or of being diagnosed with cancer or other serious conditions. We always believe that the future will be better, regardless of the odds or the current circumstances. This, according to neuroscientist Tali Sharot, is because we are naturally prewired for optimism.

In her book *The Optimism Bias*, Sharot mentions the fact that human beings possess awareness, and says that this awareness of mortality on its own would have led evolution to a dead end. The despair of imminent death would have interfered with daily function. Therefore scientists believe that, because we were given the ability to travel forwards in time in our heads, and to imagine death, the only way to ensure that the human race had the motivation to survive was to also equip us with an irrational bias for optimism. Why irrational? Because apparently our brains naturally tilt towards the positive, and, even though we are aware of the possibilities of negative and unhappy outcomes, we stay hopeful in the face of adversity. We use unrealistic optimism to alter our perceptions and actions, and in doing so we promote our own well-being.

Positive psychology

Martin Seligman is known as the father of positive psychology. He spent a lot of his life as a psychologist working with misery, depression, suicide and suffering. He noted that psychology was all about fixing what was broken but that nobody was addressing what makes life worth living. He decided that there should be a science dedicated to helping people thrive and grow. Psychology should be just as concerned with human strengths as with human weaknesses. We should be focusing on what is good in life and not just on what needs to be fixed. He didn't intend to replace psychology with positive psychology but just to create a space for it in the bigger picture. His idea was to continue to reduce misery but also to build on what he refers to as "flourishing".

Seligman believes that for a person to flourish, he or she should have:

1. Positive emotions
2. Better relationships
3. Meaning/engagement
4. Accomplishments

If all four elements are present, a person has a much greater possibility of being happy.

He also looks at our current views of what makes for a happy life and he identifies three types of happy lives:[9]

---

[9] See: http://www.ted.com/index.php/talks/martin_seligman_on_the_state_of_psychology.html.

1. The pleasant life

The pleasant life is about having as many pleasant experiences as possible, such as falling in love, going on holiday, having a party. But he refers to these experiences as predominantly "tricks" to attain as much positive emotion as you can. The pleasant life also involves learning the skills – savouring, mindfulness – that amplify the the experiences and stretch them over time and space.

2. The life of engagement

A life of engagement involves being in touch with your inner self and your highest strengths.

We sometimes refer to it as being "in the flow". It differs from the pleasant life in that the pleasant life depends on happy experiences. But knowing what your highest strengths are and recreating your life to use them will give you a much greater sense of involvement and engagement.

3. The meaningful life

The meaningful life, while similar to the life of engagement, also involves knowing your signature strength and using it to the betterment of others and in the service of something bigger than yourself.

All three types of happy life bring happiness into a person's life but the happiness attained from the pleasant life is of a more transient or temporary nature. Having a life of engagement or a meaningful life, according to studies, factors higher for happiness levels, with the meaningful life giving the best chance of true happiness.

Positive psychology for the workplace

If we take what we have learned into the context of the workplace, employers must look and see if their organisation is one that fosters these essential elements that Seligman mentions: positive emotions, good relationships, meaning, engagement and achievement. If these factors are present, employees are more likely to be living a meaningful life and therefore to be more engaged with their jobs. This "living in the flow" that accompanies the meaningful life leads to greater productivity.

There are many ways in which clever organisations try to adopt positive work practices to increase productivity. Research shows that if people are happier and more engaged in their lives and their jobs they tend to perform better. Productivity is directly affected by positivity and optimism. Effective communication, along with other work practices outlined here, can boost the morale of employees:

Effective communication: Effective communication ensures that the employee is kept informed of all processes and work practices that may concern him or her. If a worker is included in the company mission and vision, he or she is more likely to buy into them.

Flexibility: Organisations that appreciate that employees have a life outside the office are more likely to have happy employees. If they offer flexi-time and the possibility for teleworking, employees will usually feel more valued and trusted, and will stay more loyal.

Team building: Improving the communication and cooperation between co-workers can have a very positive effect on the overall atmosphere in an organisation; positive relationships can increase a person's sense of belonging.

Recognition of strengths: Focusing on and developing the key strengths of employees is a very good work practice. When individuals use their strengths they have a greater sense of belonging and living in the flow. If workers are doing jobs that don't tie in with their personal strengths, this could result in too little challenge or too much stress. It's important to match the right person to the right job.

Seligman believes that focusing on people's strengths is one of the most significant ways to encourage positivity and happiness. He acknowledges that there are also times when things will go wrong. The way people react in these circumstances is what will influence their future success. This is why part of positive psychology is the area of resilience – how to cope when bad things happen.

Resilience

The US army is confident in the abilities of Seligman. All of their drill sergeants are given positive psychology and resilience training by Seligman at the University of Pennsylvania. The idea is that the army would focus more on personal growth by teaching psychological skills to stop the fallout that often follows failure. Seligman measures resilience and teaches positive psychology to ensure the army is as fit psychologically as it is physically.

Organisations could also help themselves by helping their employees to cope in times of failure or rejection. Employees who suffer from stress and anxiety cost money. However, the question arises: If the right person is chosen for the job, would there be as large a requirement for resilience training, or would the right candidate cope in the face of adversity?

Seligman's learned helplessness studies

Seligman started his research into positive psychology with a study that focused on learned helplessness. He observed in some clinical tests that a number of animals, when subjected to minor electric shocks over which they had no control, would eventually just accept them and make no attempt to escape. Similar experiments were later carried out on humans to see how they would respond to loud noises. Three groups were used. The first group was exposed to a loud noise that they could stop by pushing a button in front of them. The second group was exposed to the same noise but nothing they did would stop the noise. The third group heard no noise. In the second set of tests, the subjects were all exposed to the loud noise but this time if they waved their arms they could turn off the noise. The people in the first and third groups all figured out how to stop the noise. But the second group typically did nothing. From failing the first time round to have any control over the noise, they assumed they would still have no control, and so they failed to act. They became passive; they had learned helplessness. The studies also uncovered that about a third of all animals and humans who are exposed to these conditions that induce helplessness never learn helplessness. The reason for this, the experts say, is optimism. Optimists think differently to pessimists; they believe that setbacks are temporary and manageable.

So, if optimists think more proactively than pessimists, surely this is the type of person we want in our lives and our companies?

Do optimistic workers make better workers?

We know that optimists try harder; they believe their attempts will make a difference; they are willing to give something a go, even if the odds are stacked against it. Pessimists, on the other hand, will think, "What's the point?" They are less likely to try as much as the optimist because they will critically assess each situation and, on the basis of logic, will deduce that the input of effort is unlikely to pay off and therefore will make fewer attempts.

What we see in real life is that the people who keep trying and who take more risks are the ones who will ultimately be more successful, in the workplace or elsewhere. As mentioned in Section 1, the self-fulfilling prophecy encourages learning from setting goals and achieving or not achieving them. Optimistic people set more goals and are more likely to learn from their mistakes due to the brain alerting them when they make a mistake or don't achieve their desired outcomes. On the other hand, the pessimist doesn't try if the statistical likelihood of failure is high. In turn, they don't learn from the valuable lessons of failure and they are less likely to succeed.

Seligman's optimism/pessimism questionnaire

In his book *Learned Optimism: How to Change Your Mind and Your Life*, Martin Seligman discusses a study he carried out with a prominent American insurance company, Metropolitan Life. The CEO of the company, John Creedon, had approached Seligman to ask him if his theories could help him hire the right type of people to sell insurance. At the time, the company hired 5,000 new insurance sales agents every year. The candidates would be tested, screened and interviewed and, once hired, trained. But the problem resided in half of these new workers quitting every year. By the fourth year, 80 per cent would have left. Creedon believed the reason for this was the difficult nature of the job, since a sales agent gets a large number of refusals each day. Each refusal can contribute to a growing negative effect on the agent. The agent would begin to delay making calls, which in turn caused their results to suffer, and eventually they quit. Creedon told Seligman that his concern was not just about loss of money through lost sales and hiring and rehiring, but that he also saw human misery and depression in the people who didn't fit the job. He wanted to know how the company could find employees to better suit the environment.

Creedon wanted to see if Seligman could use his optimism/pessimism questionnaires to pick out in advance who would make the best agents and who would be best suited for the job and industry.

Seligman believed that optimists were better able to handle the refusals and therefore would be better suited to this sort of job. He believed that being an optimist wouldn't affect what the agents would say to the customers or their ability to sell, but that it would change the way they would speak to themselves in the context of failure. A pessimist is more likely to say "I'm no good at sales" or "Nobody wants to buy from me", whereas the optimist speaks to themselves in a more constructive way, for example, "He was probably too busy at the time" or "She was happy with her current insurance."

Seligman started by testing the current insurance agents to try and see their level of optimism. They took 200 sales agents, half of whom were productive and the other half unproductive. The results were as he expected – the productive workers all scored highly on the optimism scale.

The traditional view of success says that we must have two ingredients for success. The ability or aptitude and the motivation to succeed; if you lack one or the other you will find it more difficult to succeed. Seligman adds another ingredient – persistence. He believes that success requires persistence or the ability to not give up when times are tough. His view is that the optimist's style of analysing past events and giving them a positive or hopeful stance is what helps him or her to succeed in a challenging environment. He believes that in the insurance sales industry, one of the toughest businesses to work in, in order to succeed you would need the aptitude, the desire or motivation, and the persistence to keep going.

Seligman went on to run these studies, and started to test industry applicants before they were hired. His optimism tests were administered to the applicants with other industry standard tests to try and ascertain suitability to the job and industry. The results all correlated with what was expected. When agents scored higher on the basis of their optimism levels, they performed better and lasted longer in the industry. He deduced from this that, in order to choose people for success in a challenging job, you needed to select them based on three characteristics: 1. Aptitude; 2. Motivation; 3. Optimism.

So, should we be trying to create more optimists in the workplace?

In his book *Learned Optimism*, Seligman also looked at whether pessimists have a role in the workplace. Although optimists are happier and more successful, they are also greater risk takers and, as mentioned previously in this chapter, perhaps more irrational. Is always looking at the bright side of life unrealistic? Does optimism oppose truth? Evidence shows that people who are depressed are generally wiser; they lack the optimism factor and therefore see things as they really are.

Seligman concluded that there is a place for pessimists, because they dampen unrealistic enthusiasm and put a more realistic slant on things. The reality is that companies probably work better with both types of people. As long as the pessimists are kept away from roles such as sales, they have a significant part to play.

On a larger scale, the health of an organisation and a nation can be positively influenced by optimism. If positive relationships and emotions, more meaning and engagement, and accomplishments were attainable for more citizens, this would lead to the increased well-being, not just of our organisations, but of the nation overall. If we could increase our optimism as a society, it would lead to:

1. Fewer health problems

2. Less aggression and crime

3. Higher productivity

The good news

The good news is that it is possible to learn optimism, improve the quality of our lives, and advance the health and well-being of the nation as a whole. It starts with awareness – knowing and becoming more conscious of our thoughts and whether they are predominantly positive or negative. There are many techniques that can be used to challenge resident beliefs and behaviours. By learning the skill of how to argue with yourself and dispute your normal way of thinking, you can teach yourself a more optimistic outlook, and reap the numerous benefits of taking the optimistic stance.

Productivity tips from Section 6 – Positivity

1. Recognise your signature strengths.
2. Use your strengths for the greater good.
3. Become aware of how you react in difficult times.
4. Try to look at unfortunate events in a more temporary fashion.
5. Set goals and learn from your failures.

section 7 – maintaining the flow

12

the power of focus

how focus can get you what you want

"He who chases two rabbits catches none."

– Confucius

The great philosopher Confucius (born c. 551 BC) knew the power of focus when he said, "The man who chases two rabbits catches none."

A large percentage of the earth's population spends a vast portion of their day chasing rabbits, jumping from one task to the next and never achieving what they could or should achieve each day.

To demonstrate this, take a look at what you set out to do today. Did you achieve it? Did you at least achieve some of it? Great, well done if you did! But could you have achieved more? Were there tasks that you did that you could have left to another day? Were there tasks you did that somebody else could have done for you? Were there tasks you didn't do that should have been done?

I dare to surmise that the vast majority of you are not getting done what you want to get done daily. One of the chief reasons that people don't achieve their goals and desires is because they lack focus; they lack the knowledge of a system to enable them to reach their desired destination in life – Success. We know success comes in many shapes and sizes and that it means different things to different people, but ultimately we all wish to succeed. Be it a successful career, a more fulfilling family life, or a healthy eating and exercise regime, regardless of what success means to you, the key to achieving success is focus and persistence.

"Your focus determines your reality"

When it comes down to it, to quote Qui-Gon Jinn in *Star Wars*, "Your focus determines your reality." What you put emphasis on in life is what your life becomes. Winners never focus on when they have lost; successful people always focus on their success. It is essential to spend time and focus on what it is you want in life and not the contrary.

Tennis star Pete Sampras is known as the "King of the Swing". Pete had one goal in life – to become the best tennis player in the world. Pete's vision allowed him to have a rigid focus. An athlete like Pete is 100 per cent clear about what it is he wants to accomplish, and having this clarity of vision assists with the endurance to remain focused.

Without focus we can never be productive, but what we sometimes forget is that focusing on the wrong things can be as detrimental to success as not focusing on anything at all. This is why goal setting and understanding our vision and mission is paramount, not only to getting things done but also to completing the tasks we need to do, and achieving the things that we actually want to achieve in life.

Before we look at what we can do to become more focused, let us see exactly where we are currently focusing our attention. Are we stressed because we have too much work to do or is it because we are not focusing on the most important work at the right time? All too often people get stressed or overwhelmed by work simply because they are not doing the work that needs to be done, or they are spending too much time on unnecessary tasks.

Focus on your goals

We now know that goal setting is the first step to being a productive individual, since it allows us to see whether we are spending our days doing things that are getting us closer to happiness or success in life. If you have no goals, you will be more prone to floating through life, and perhaps you will become part of someone else's vision or goals. Clarifying your own goals gives you a positive focus. Having positive and exciting goals leads to greater focus.

Darwin would not have written *The Origin of the Species* without focus; Da Vinci would not have completed the Mona Lisa without focus; and Carl Lewis would not have won nine Olympic goals medals without focus. These are exceptional people who didn't allow their focus to be diverted to any other task. Their vision was so strong that they persisted and endured the commitment to pursue their goals. The rest of us mere mortals continuously make an effort to improve, to remain more focused and dedicated to our goals, and to try and eliminate distractions and disruptions to our focus.

The reality is that, if we lose focus, we generally lose the goal. Every year millions of people around the world decide they want to get fit. They sign up for gyms; they commit to going running; they decide they are going to do a whole bunch of things. Then, in a matter of months, or even weeks, they give up. This is more than likely a gradual shift away from their new-found goal, rather than a conscious aban-donment of it. There are two main reasons why a large percentage of goal setters fail. First, they haven't been clear about what they want to achieve. "I want to get fit" isn't a clear enough goal. Why? Because what does being fit mean to you? To some people being fit means running a marathon; others would be delighted with being able to run 2 km. Goals must be specific. You must state what being fit is to you. You must have a measurement so that you will know if you have achieved your goal or not. The other reason that people fail, in relation to this example, is that their focus shifts. On day one, all you can think about is running. You buy new running clothes and new runners, and this feels great. Day by day, week by week, the goal fades into the background. The new habit hasn't yet been formed so that the pressure to revert to bad habits is there and strong. If you remain focused and place reminders of the benefits of the goal around you, you will be a lot more likely to stay committed to your goal and ultimately achieve it.

Focus on the positive

I was initially exposed to the concept of focusing on the positive through reading Mark Victor Hansen and Robert G. Allen's *The One-Minute Millionaire*. The story is about a newly widowed woman's struggle to come up with $1 million in cash to get her two children back from her in-laws. One of the concepts in the book is the idea that you cannot afford any negative thoughts. When the woman felt defeated, she just had to pick herself up because her children were at risk. But allowing herself to have any negative thoughts meant that she would not reach her goal of $1 million. A technique suggested in the book to discourage negative thoughts is to wear an elastic band around your wrist and flick it every time you have a negative thought, thus making yourself consciously aware of when you are having pessimistic or unconstructive thoughts. This process encourages you to focus on what you want, as opposed to what you don't want. You will find your goals will be realised much more quickly if you follow this advice.

Focus on your strengths

If you focus positively on your strengths and natural talents, you are in a much more powerful position to achieve your goals. What strengths and talents do you have that may contribute to the achievement of your goals?

Focus on positive habits

If what you focus your time and your thoughts on determines your future, then your daily habits are going to determine your future. The daily choices that you make are the choices that determine your future. If this is so, you must commit to creating and forming good positive habits. Life doesn't just happen; you are an active participant in your life, and whatever you choose to do with your life or whatever you choose to focus your energy on will determine your future. So your daily behaviours and habits should be positive ones in order to make that future a positive and successful one.

Focus on the present

One of the mistakes many people make when goal setting is to focus too much on the future, when the goal that they have set will be realised. This will not help you to achieve your goal any quicker, nor is it a healthy habit for life. To have a happy and fulfilling life you need to focus on the present. The present is all you have. The past is gone; the future is unknown. Now is all we have. As Eckhart Tolle describes it in his bestseller *The Power of Now*: "When we embrace and accept this curious truth our lives will be fuller, richer and more real. Yes, we still have to spend some time visualising our goals and projecting ourselves into the future to plan and schedule, but when the planning is done, we return to our lives which are happening now in the wonderful present."

This concept is in tune with the concept of letting go. Many goal-setting experts will coach on how to set powerful and effective goals, but will also advocate the concept of letting go. This letting go is not to be confused with not doing anything. If your goal is to write a book and then you sit back and hope that somehow it is going to get written without your hard work and dedication, it will never happen. Letting go means that you don't spend countless hours thinking, worrying or stressing about who is going to publish it, who will buy it and where will it be sold. Set the goal, do the work required and then come back to the now. Live your life in the present.

One question I get regularly asked is: Should I not only set one goal? If the power of focus is so important, surely if I set more than one goal, my focus will be split and not as effective?

The answer to this depends on what your goals are and what it is you want to achieve, but let's take Pete Sampras or golfer Padraig Harrington as our examples. These men had one goal – to be the best they could be in their sport. Everything else took second place. This is not to say that they have never set other goals in different areas of their lives. We all have to consider our own life priorities. My main goal for this year is to finish this book and get a book deal. I set five goals each year, but finishing and getting this book published is my priority this year. This doesn't take from my fitness and health goals that I set every year. I also set financial goals and personal goals for my home and family, but my priority remains my book. Many of the decisions I make will revolve around writing and researching. I have a budget for buying books (I need to or I would spend all my money on Amazon. com or in my local bookshop), but if I see a book that would help me with my research I won't stick to my budget because my book is my priority. Sometimes my fitness will suffer if I skip an exercise session to continue writing because I am in "the zone"!

So you don't have to limit yourself to one goal yearly. However, a useful exercise is to ask yourself what one thing needs to happen to make this year your best year to date. This then becomes your star goal, your main focus.

In order to get things done and achieve what needs to be realised, we must stay focused on the job at hand. Setting the goal is the first step, so that we know what it is we want to achieve and that we stay on track to achieve it. A commitment to realising our goals will be supported by our not get sidetracked by another job or task. Working on two projects at once or multi-tasking does not work; the time it takes to switch your brain from one task to the other is time wasted. The other main ingredient to remaining focused is to eliminate the distractions or the barriers to staying focused. Being aware of what has the potential to distract you is half the battle; the other half is actually working to rid your life of these wicked diversions, where possible.

13

enemies to focus

tackling elephants, eating frogs and other enemies to focus

> "Most barriers to your success are man-
> made. And most often, you're the man
> who made them."
>
> – Frank Tyger

We know that to be productive you must maintain your focus at all times. This can be very difficult with the amount of disruptions most of us experience on a daily basis. We are constantly being disturbed by our email, our mobile phones, our colleagues and our boss, and by the voice we can't seem to shut out – our inner dialogue.

In Brian Tracy's bestselling book *Eat That Frog*, he explains the old saying which states that if the first thing you do in the morning is to eat a live frog, you'll have the satisfaction of knowing that it's probably the worst thing you will do all day. The purpose of this is to avoid procrastinating and to take on the tasks we don't like or don't want to do.

Procrastination – what causes it?

Procrastination is one of the biggest enemies to focus and productivity, and there are many reasons why people procrastinate. Probably one of the chief reasons for procrastination is lack of vision.

Lack of vision

If we do not know where we are going, how can we possibly get there? It can never be said too often that clarity of purpose and vision is perhaps one of the most important ingredients for personal productivity. We are much more likely to work productively and get things done when we know that the outcome is taking us towards our goals and vision. If you haven't set goals you will waste a lot of time thinking about priorities and trying to decide which task is more important. Goals can help reduce this ambiguity by giving you certainty.

Beliefs

A colleague of mine told me about a client who asked him to coach an employee who was performing very badly in sales. The employee appeared to be doing everything but picking up the phone to make his sales calls. After speaking to the guy for less than an hour, my colleague found out that the guy had the following belief - "Selling is bad." Unfortunately this is not a good belief to hold if you are a sales person and you are expected to make sales as part of your job description.

My colleague worked with him to try and find a benefit in what he was selling to his clients. By the end of his coaching, he believed he was helping people by selling them his product and no longer had any problems trying to sell.

Lots of people hate sales; they shudder at the thought of trying to sell something to someone. This is generally due to a belief they hold about the sales process, and it may or may not be something they are aware of. Awareness will help every time. It is possible to change your beliefs but first you must identify what your beliefs are.

Tiredness

Regular breaks prevent you from becoming too tired and keep you sharp and focused. Breaks should be encouraged as they can enhance productivity levels. Employers are often terrified of the effects of the internet on the productivity of employees. Many have banned social networking sites like Facebook, as it was estimated that time spent on these websites (average: thirty minutes a day = three weeks per year) was costing UK businesses £6.5 million annually in lost productivity.[10]

But maybe employers should be looking at this phenomenon from a different angle. Employees are often expected to bring work home and be constantly in connection with work and clients through email and BlackBerrys, etc. They mix their work life with their personal life, so maybe it's not too much to ask to allow them to bring a little bit of their personal lives to work. Short breaks spent on Facebook can help to revitalise the worker and make them ready for another session of work. Of course, these breaks must have a time limit and you should be able to trust your workers to keep to the allocated times.

Fears

Fear can be a contributing factor to procrastination. Sometimes fear of failure, and sometimes fear of success, can prevent us from doing the things we know we should be doing. If an individual sees a task as being beyond their capabilities, they will avoid the task to the point where they

---

[10] See Bernhard Warner, "Is Social Networking a Waste of Time?" www. thetimes.co.uk, 12 March 2008.

hope it will no longer matter or be their responsibility. A much healthier attitude in this scenario would be to face the fear and look for help. If the task is outside your personal skills, you will need to get assistance or go and learn what you need to know to complete the task.

It might seem strange that someone could be afraid of success, but it's what success brings with it that may be causing the fear or anxiety.

Many times we fear the outcome of an event and this is why we avoid doing it. So ask yourself, what is the worst that can happen? More often than not, you will realise that even if the worst were to happen it is probably not as bad as not performing the task at all.

Lack of time

Lack of time usually turns out to be lack of organisation or prioritisation. If you can honestly say that you couldn't be even 10 per cent more efficient with your time, then you will need to get someone to help you with your workload or to simply offload some of the work you need to get done.

Usually there is scope for everyone to improve their efficiency. Careful analysis of how you are spending your time usually reveals time that can be reallocated to more productive things.

Feeling overwhelmed

People regularly feel overwhelmed by the enormity of a task or by the quantity of tasks they need to get done. This can lead to stagnation or procrastination, when they don't know where or how to start. Whether it is many tasks or one big one, the best solution is to break it down and to consider what you need to do, one part at a time.

Laziness

I'm afraid I can do nothing about your laziness, if this is a problem for you, but I can offer one piece of advice: Don't complain about having a big workload because nobody will listen!

And the most important productivity tip for procrastinators is to simply *make a start*.

Procrastination is not good for the soul. We can never hope to complete all the tasks we have waiting for us. Therefore, if you have to procrastinate, try and make sure that you procrastinate about the unimportant stuff and get the important stuff done.

Procrastination – how to avoid it

Setting goals and knowing your motivations

Goal setting is a habit all highly successful and effective people share. By setting goals and having a personal or professional vision or mission, you are much more likely to keep on track and stay inspired. Know what your motivations are, and, to stress Stephen Covey's advice – "Always begin with the end in mind."

If you know your reasons and your motivations for doing a certain task, you will be more encouraged to complete it. This point holds for employees, so it is vital that a good leader makes the company mission and vision clear and visible to all workers. Take the example of the two stonecutters building a cathedral. Each is working on a single piece of stone. The first does not look beyond the task of simply cutting stone. His body language is negative; he is bored and uninspired. The second stonecutter, who is enthusiastic and stimulated by his work, has in his mind the vision of building a cathedral. Knowing your motivations will add greatly to your sense of purpose. Be aware of your vision and share it at all times.

Plan and schedule

> "If we fail to plan, we plan to fail."
>
> – Peter Drucker

If you plan and set out your work at the beginning of a day, you are less likely to fall victim to distractions. Yes, stuff will happen but, like a football team when things happen on the pitch, don't lose sight of the game plan. Priorities will change as the day progresses, but if we don't have a game plan we will never achieve what we need to achieve. By taking time to plan we will save time and induce focus.

Remember, in the planning phase of work, you are doing just that – planning and scheduling. Do not get distracted and attempt to do any of the work. If we start to do pieces of the work and jump from the task at hand, which is planning, this will have an overall negative effect. When the work is planned and a workable system is in place, we will feel more in control and more capable of keeping our focus on what we are currently doing. Before you plan each day's or each week's work, it is a good idea to brainstorm all the things that you must do for that day or that week in advance so that these items can also be planned and entered into your calendar or to-do list.

Worst first

In Brian Tracy's *Eat That Frog*, the metaphor in the title is for tackling the most difficult or challenging tasks of the day first. These are the tasks that you usually avoid and try to ignore, pretending they don't exist. We usually tell ourselves things like "I'll start with a few of these short and easy tasks. Then, when I'm in the flow of work, I'll tackle the frog." This would have been the type of self-talk that went on in my head previously. But the freedom and satisfaction from clearing those tasks out of your way early in the day is immense. Once the task has been ticked off the to-do list, you will feel lighter, satisfied and more in control.

Tackling the elephant

An "elephant task", by its name, is obviously one that overwhelms us in its enormity. To approach such a task, we have to implement project management skills by setting milestones or breaking down the elephant into edible parts (yuck!). In order to achieve what you want to achieve, you must, as previously mentioned, "Start with the end in mind." But sometimes the end can seem too far away and we can become de-motivated or distracted as the task seems too overwhelming. The best way to stay on track is to look at the next step you have to take and schedule it. Think of building a cathedral, while just planning the next stone to be cut. Having the vision of the cathedral in mind will help you to stay motivated, but focussing on the next stone means planning your next action or next step without worrying about everything else that has to happen to get you to the final outcome. It is important to "zoom in" and "zoom out" in terms of your perception of large tasks. Zoom in to take things step by step, and then, at intervals, zoom out and make sure that you are doing everything you need to be doing to complete the task on time and within budget.

Flexibility

It is important to remember that people are productive at different times of the day. As an employer or manager, be open to allow them to work in a manner that suits them. Don't schedule difficult tasks for them that they may perform better at a different time of the day. Consult with them and try to find out their best and worst periods in the day for productivity. Ask for their opinion and be flexible. A worker is going to be more productive if they are not worried or stressed about home priorities; so if you know that a worker has something personal they need to attend to, maybe you should let them do it, so that they will no longer be distracted and can focus on the job 100 per cent. Employers can be too focused on time-based working habits rather than those that are task based. Task-based work can work to the advantage of both the employer and the employee.

Eliminate the distractions

Check email at set intervals

As mentioned in Chapter 9, don't allow yourself to be distracted every time a new email arrives. Switch off all email notifications. Imagine the postman were to ring your door bell every time a letter arrived in the post office for you during the day. Think of email in the same way. Set periods during the day for email processing – two or three times a day should be sufficient. If you work in an industry where emails are crucial, you can put a notification in your email signature advising people of the times that you process your email. If they need to contact you urgently, ask them to pick up the phone. Stay in control of your inbox – don't let it control you!

Leave instructions on your voicemail

If you are out of the office or on holiday, don't forget to leave a message on your voicemail asking people to send you an email if there is something that requires your attention, and not to leave you a voicemail (this will minimise the amount of catch-up you need to do when you return).

De-clutter

Clutter, as Barbara Hemphill describes it, is postponed decisions. I love this explanation because it always inspires me to do something about my clutter. Having postponed decisions adds to the confusion and chaos of the mind. De-cluttering and organising your environment will be a boon to your productivity.

Closed-door policy

Contrary to many workplaces and leadership thinking, the closed-door policy can be very beneficial for your productivity, and invaluable for focus. Advise people not to disturb you at certain times of the day; block out times in your calendar and ask not to be disturbed. Watch how your productivity will soar. If you have a project to work on or a deadline to meet, this is the best way to ensure that the work will get done. An alternative to this would be to work from home.

Be assertive

Very often a person's level of productivity and stress are directly related to their ability or inability to say no. Interruptions are a key factor in reducing the amount of work we can get done in any given time. One of the biggest and most commonly voiced complaints by people who are overworked is: "I'm constantly being interrupted."

Does the following scenario sound familiar?

Colleague: Do you have a minute?

You: Yes, of course, come in.

Now, whether that minute remains a minute or turns into thirty minutes, the effects are the same – your focus has been disturbed.

So, what can you do about it? Simply don't allow others to affect your productivity and ruin your flow. If somebody disturbs you mid-task and looks for your help or assistance, stop and think about what you will have to sacrifice in order to facilitate this person. Yes, it is nice to be helpful, but if saying yes to somebody else's needs means that you won't get home in time to read your child's bedtime story, then maybe you will be more likely to say no. Very often people don't think of their own requirements or needs, and instinctively say yes whenever they are asked for help. Next time stop and think about the consequences. If it is not going to affect your life negatively, by all means say yes.

How can you limit the amount of interruptions? Schedule in "Do not disturb" time. If your team know that you are busy every day between 10.00 a.m. and 12.00 p.m. writing reports, they are more likely to reduce their interruptions during this period. Alternatively, you can have a period daily when your work colleagues know you are available for consultations.

If you are a manager, a good thing to do is to give your team more autonomy and responsibility so that not everything has to be run by you. Let them know to what level they can make decisions without referring them to you.

And always ask yourself the question: "If I say yes, what do I say no to?" Because every action has a consequence or reaction.

Avoid the internet

Now here is a difficult one – avoid the internet. Do you remember the days when you went to work and the whole world wasn't a double click away? The internet has made our lives so much easier, but it has also made focusing on the job at hand potential hell. The internet facilitates the constant temptation to follow through on a thought wave. Too easily we can go from being 100 per cent focused to spending an hour buying books on Amazon.co.uk. Not that this has ever happened to me! The internet is our curse and our saviour.

If you are a disciplined person, you can commit to the task you are doing for the next couple of hours and you won't be so easily distracted by the internet for any significant amount of time. If you can't trust yourself then you will have to take the totalitarian approach and disconnect from the internet at times when you are trying to stay focused. Turning off your phone at this stage may also be a help.

If the internet is where you need to be, that is if you need to have an internet presence through sites such as LinkedIn, Twitter or Facebook, how do you limit the distractions? Scheduling social networking time each week can help, as long as you move onto another task once your time is up.

Time perspective

Another two enemies to focus are Mr Future and Mr Past. What might happen and what did happen often occupies much of our thoughts, but we must remember not to let the past and the future take up too much of our thinking time, taking from our current focus.

We all have a natural time perspective. Some people live their lives in the past, mulling over memories and what could have been. Others live their lives in the future, delaying gratification to reap the harvest in the future. A third type lives for the present and doesn't waste energy worrying about the future or dwelling on the past. They live in the now.

Obviously it is not healthy to have only one time perspective in your life – too much of one thing is never good for you. Even though it appears that living in the now is the best time perspective to live your life by, it is not always healthy if left to its own devices. As we know, it is important to plan or schedule for your future and also to look back and learn from your past and past mistakes. So, as with most things in life, a balanced approach to time perspective is the ideal.

We should always try to focus on the now, while giving the past and the future their deserved attention. Remember, if you focus on the present, you do still have the ability to change the future. Don't pre-empt what hasn't happened and don't waste time thinking about it. Use your time effectively, and make it work to your advantage. You have the power to change things now. So remember, focus is all about *now*. If your thoughts wander, try to bring them back to the present. Focusing on your breathing can help you to quieten the mind and bring it back to the now.

If you practise this activity of being in the present, not only will it help your focus and help you to work more effectively, it will greatly reduce stress and anxiety levels. Bad stress is a great friend of the future. It thrives on the future and our analytical mind allows it to survive. Stress cannot survive long if you truly focus on the present.

Eliminate time-wasting activities

Some of the typical errors people make, which maintain the fallacy of "I don't have time..."

1. Typing your email signature over and over – stop and create a template signature.
2. Retyping a company sales pitch or company mission time and time again – copy and paste from a Word file or use text replacement software which allows you to replace chunks of text with one keystroke (fantastic invention). Check out www.shortkeys.com.

3. Typing individuals' names and addresses in letters – set up a mail merge.

4. Typing full email addresses – store contacts in Outlook or a similar email program.

5. Looking for documents time and time again – set up a clear and concise filing system where documents can be found and retrieved easily.

14

positive habits

exercise, meditation and being an early bird

> "We are what we repeatedly do.
> Excellence, then, is not an act, but a habit."
>
> – Aristotle

Meditation

Meditate for focus

Not too long ago, meditation was perceived as being for monks and the religiously devout. Today, meditation is a powerful tool that is used by many highly successful people. One of the reasons for this is because meditation helps to calm the mind and allows the individual to focus more readily and effectively.

Meditation is commonly known as the cure for the "monkey mind" – where our mind swings from thought to thought as a monkey from branch to branch. We have so many thoughts in our heads at any given time, and rarely do we get the chance to stop the chatter and the noise and just *be*.

Meditation works by emptying the conscious mind of this incessant dialogue. You do this by directing your thoughts away from yourself and your problems, and focusing your attention on a particular point of reference.

How can meditation help me?

Meditation is regularly used for stress relief and anxiety, but it is also becoming a recognised formula used by successful people, both for problem solving and for the realisation of goals.

Regular meditation can improve your ability to prioritise and manage tasks and goals. It will also give you the ability to focus on specific information and will help you to stay more focused and alert. When you master the power to maintain focus during meditation, this skill can be easily transferred and used in your work life.

Meditation can be a very powerful and empowering tool when used regularly. Top business men and world leaders use meditation and visualisation to get the necessary results required of them in this ever-changing and challenging world.

It can be surprising the quantity and the quality of "Ah ha!" moments you will encounter when you begin to meditate. Life takes on another dimension with meditation; it allows you to tap into your subconscious, creative mind and ideas and possibilities are released.

Meditation doesn't always bring immediate results, but it always brings positive ones. So many meaningful coincidences will start to enter your life, and, if you are open and aware, these coincidences will bring opportunities.

Starting to meditate

The best way to start to meditate, as with any new behaviour, is to set a goal. I would recommend starting small and building up your practise of meditation. If you can commit initially to ten minutes per day for twenty-one consecutive days, you will have formed a positive habit.

How to meditate

There are many forms of meditation, depending on your motivations for meditation. One of the simplest forms, and that easiest for the beginner, is a breathing meditation.

Choose a quiet place to meditate and sit in a comfortable position. You can sit in the traditional cross-legged posture on the floor, in a chair or in any other position that is comfortable. The most important thing is to keep your back straight to prevent your mind from becoming sleepy.

Close your eyes and turn your attention to your breathing. Breathe naturally through your nose. Do not attempt to control your breath. Become aware of the sensation of the breath as it enters and leaves the nostrils. This sensation is the object of meditation.

At first, your mind will be very busy, and you might even feel that the meditation is making your mind busier; but in reality you are just becoming more aware of how busy your mind actually is. Allow the thoughts to come and pass. There will be a great temptation to follow the different thoughts as they arise, but you should resist this and remain focused on the sensation of breathing. If you discover that your mind has wandered and is following your thoughts, you should gently return your thoughts to your breath. Repeat this as many times as necessary until the mind settles on the breath. Remember, it is perfectly normal to have thoughts during meditation. Your goal is not to stop thinking, because this is impossible for the human mind. Your goal is to focus your mind on a particular area, in this case your breath. You will notice that, the more you practise meditation, the gap between your thoughts will get bigger. It is in this gap that you are in your true form, connected to the essence of who you are. It is in this gap that great things will start to happen.

Take a look at Deepak Chopra's website (www.chopra. com) to get great tips on how to start meditation. There are lots of different types and you don't have to settle for just one. You may like to do mantra meditations (chanting words or phrases in your head), breath meditations or chakra meditations. All are beneficial, so it's up to you to find what works for you.

Exercise

> "Standing on your tip toes, running on the spot, exercise is good for you, laziness is not!"
>
> – Bungo Womble

Richard Branson believes that working out gives him at least four hours of additional productivity every day. We have all heard advice on the benefits of eating healthily and exercising, but when it comes from one of the world's most accomplished business people, I think maybe it's time to sit up and take notice.

Healthy body, healthy mind

The Romans had a proverb: "Mens sana in corpore sano" ("A sound mind in a healthy body"). As we know, there are many benefits of exercise but how do they relate to focus and productivity?

Exercise can improve health and prevent certain diseases. Health, as opposed to illness, in itself allows a person to get more done and not be distracted by the necessity of medicating and worrying about healing. Exercise stimulates certain brain chemicals that can keep you feeling relaxed and happy. It contributes to psychological well-being. As long as it is not done too close to bedtime, exercise can help people to fall asleep quicker and stay asleep longer. Exercise improves cardiovascular flow; if your blood is circulating more efficiently in your body, this will lead you to have more energy.

Happy, relaxed, rested, healthy, stress-free individuals with energy are more likely to concentrate and stay focused for longer. Fit people usually make productive people.

How to start exercising

If you are not already a person who exercises on a regular basis, it's time to reconsider. Exercise not only prolongs your life, but it also helps you to make that life happier, calmer and more successful.

Like meditation, if you are going to start a new habit, start small. Choose an exercise you like or at least one that doesn't make your stomach churn every time you say the word. Many people opt for the gym because they think if you want to get fit you need to go to the gym. This is not true; there are many other possibilities. Walking or cycling is a good place to start. Consider going back to a sport you used to play when you were younger. Try as much as possible to make exercise fun.

I used to run but my knees eventually said "Stop!" So I bought myself an exercise bike. I took to the bike reluctantly every morning until I decided to make this thirty minutes more enjoyable and, as it turned out, educational. I now position my bike in front of my laptop and watch documentaries from www.topdocumentaryfilms.com. Thirty minutes now passes too quickly!

Join the ranks of the highly successful and make exercise a part of your regime. Commit to a ten- or twenty-minute walk everyday to get started. You can gradually increase that or add strength and flexibility exercises to your regime. The important thing is to get started and establish a routine.

What about the excuse "I don't have time to exercise"? True, if you live a normally busy life of working and raising children, it is difficult to squeeze it in. According to the Irish Heart Foundation it takes thirty minutes of aerobic exercise most days to stay fit and healthy. This can include brisk walking and doesn't have to be done all at once.

Consider walking to the train station or bus stop; get off a stop before your usual stop. Two fifteen-minute walks is enough to get started. It is easy to fit exercise in if you are committed to including it in your life. Consider not slouching in front of the TV in the evening – maybe you can find a half hour here! What about joining a club where working out is fun? Swimming before you go to work?

There are many ways to include exercise in your life, but the way that worked for me, and which appears to be a habit with many successful people, is to go by the philosophy...

The early bird catches the worm

Getting up early is a habit practised by many of the greats. If you get up early, you will have time to do all the things you wouldn't otherwise have time to do: exercise, meditation, journaling, thinking or simply getting organised for your day.

Benefits of rising early

- **Quiet time at home or at the office**: Rising early gives you extra time in the morning to experience silence and stillness. You can use this time to just be, or to get work done without being disturbed.

- **Time for activities you don't normally have time for**: Many people use the excuse of "I don't have time" to avoid exercising. A morning exercise routine is one of the best things you can do for your physical and mental health and fitness. Not only does exercise help to strengthen your body, but it also relieves stress, gives you more energy and reduces the risk of depression and anxiety. Exercise in the morning contributes to a more energy-filled, happier day.

- **Get a head start; stay ahead of the competition:** Getting up early gives you the edge; it allows you to get an extra hour or two of work done before the competition have put their feet on the floor. Regardless of whether you work in an office or at home, whether the competition takes the form of your professional rivals or your children, getting up before them will keep you one step ahead.

- **Miss the traffic:** School holidays are great, even if you are not a teacher. There is less traffic on the road, so you get to work more quickly and you are more relaxed. Why not experience that every day by getting up an hour or two earlier and driving before the masses hit the tarmac?

- **Experience stillness; see the sun rise**: The morning is a special, calm time. It is the one time of the day you are guaranteed no interruptions or disturbances. Watching the sun rise can help you feel gratitude for being alive and well.

- **Always arrive on time**: Rising early also contributes to the likelihood of you arriving on time to your destination, be it the office or a meeting. Wouldn't you like to always arrive on time? If you are in control of the clock, you will not be stressed out.

- **More creativity**: Most people find that they are more creative in the early morning. Since it is usually a quiet time, it allows for people to tap into their creativity undisturbed.

- **Join the ranks of the great men and women of history:** Right down through the ages, great men and women of history rose early. Rising early seems to be synonymous with greatness. You don't read about any of the people who changed history lounging about under the covers!

- **Live longer:** We spend on average a third of our lives asleep – fifty-six hours a week, which is more than two days. If you want to experience more life, sleep less.

Maintaining positive habits

> "Habit, if not resisted, soon becomes necessity."
>
> – St Augustine

Creating positive habits is one of the best methods to ensure success in our lives. Whether it's a habit of exercise, meditation or simply living in the present, the more we make it a part of our lives the sooner we will reap the benefits. It is said that it is our collective habits that determine the quality of our life, so it is important to ensure that our habits are ones that allow us to live a happy, healthy and fulfilled life.

What's your objective?

Start by knowing your objectives. If you have set yourself a goal to lose weight, why do you want to lose weight? Is it for health reasons, to attract a partner, to improve your confidence and self-esteem? Knowing your exact motivations will assist you with your motivation when you experience a slump or lack of inspiration.

Start small

When creating a new habit, always start small. Starting small makes it much easier to create momentum and carry out the new habit daily. If you want to start running, commit to just ten minutes a day. You can gradually increase this as the ten minutes becomes easy for you to do. One of the biggest factors when creating new habits is the time element. People say they don't have time to exercise or meditate, etc., but everyone can find ten minutes.

One at a time

Introduce one habit at a time. If you want to start running and yoga, choose one to start with. Trying too many things at once is a recipe for disaster. If you have only one new habit to focus on, you are much more likely to find the time. If, after a month, you are happy that the new habit has become a part of your life, begin the next habit and start small.

Triggers

It is recommended, when starting a new habit, to do it at the same time every day and to use a trigger to get started. A trigger is an activity or event that comes before the new habit, for example having a cup of coffee in the morning before you do your yoga, or going to the toilet when you wake up before you do your meditation. Deepak Chopra does 21-day meditation challenges regularly and one of the teachers described his trigger as RPM (rise, pee, meditate).

Focus on the positive

If you find the new habit difficult or boring, focus on the positive. If you are out running, don't allow yourself to be negative and say things like "This is painful", "I'm exhausted" or "It's so boring." Have a more positive attitude and encourage yourself: "Well done for getting out here again", "I'm half way there", "I'm going to be so proud of myself when this is completed." It's very easy to change the way you think about something if you are assertive enough to change your thoughts.

Set yourself a challenge

Just like the 21-day meditation challenges I have done in the past, a challenge will give you a clear goal to work towards. Rather than saying, "I'm going to meditate every morning for the rest of my life," say, "I'm going to commit to this for the month of December." It's much easier to work towards a goal of thirty days than a goal of thirty years!

They say that repeatedly doing an action for twenty-one to thirty days creates new neural pathways in the brain. This is why it takes a least three weeks to create a new habit. So try to keep your new habit up for that long and see if your brain accepts it as part of who you are, and, as St Augustine said, it will soon become a necessity.

Productivity tips from Section 7 – Maintaining the Flow

1. Focus on your goals.
2. Focus on the positive.
3. Focus on your strengths.
4. Remain present.
5. Take regular breaks.
6. Schedule to avoid procrastination.
7. Break work down into bite-size chunks.
8. Practise a closed-door policy at times.
9. Be assertive.
10. Eliminate time-wasting activities.
11. Get up early.

final word

Many people don't realise that the word "productive" is synonymous with "creative". We see productivity as being mundane, structured and restrictive, whereas the reality is the opposite. Productivity allows us the freedom to live our lives in a more creative way. It clears the way for inventive and imaginative opportunities. It ensures that things happen and get done. It allows for calm and control. Introducing practices into your life that increase your productivity will be a proactive step in the right direction, a step that will turn your personal chaos into relaxed, organised control.

Good Luck.

bibliography

Agness, L., *Change Your Life with NLP: The Powerful Way to Make Your Whole Life Better*, UK: Pearson Prentice Hall Life, 2008.

Allen, D., *Getting Things Done: How to Achieve Stress-Free Productivity*, UK: Piatkus Books, 2008.

Allen, D., *Making It All Work: Winning at the Game of Work and the Business of Life*, UK: Piatkus Books, 2008.

Anderson, J.A., "Productivity, Screens and Aspect Ratios: A Comparison of Single, Traditional Aspect, Dual Traditional Aspect, and Single Widescreen Aspect Computer Displays Over Simulated Office Tasks across Performance and Usability", CIC Report 200719, Salt Lake City, UT: CIC, 2007.

Colbert, B., *The Happiness Habit: Choose the Path to a Better Life*, Dublin: Gill and Macmillan, 2010.

Covey, S., *The Seven Habits of Highly Effective People: Powerful Lessons in Personal Change*, UK: Simon and Schuster, 2004.

Chopra, D., *Synchrodestiny: Harnessing the Infinite Power of Coincidence to Create Miracles*, UK: Random House, 2004.

Egli R., *The LOLA-Principle: The Perfectness of the World*, Switzerland: Editions D'olt, 2002.

Ferriss, T. *The 4-Hour Body: The Secrets and Science of Rapid Body Transformation*, UK: Vermilion, 2011.

Ferriss, T., *The 4-Hour Work Week: Escape the 9–5, Live Anywhere and Join the New Rich*, UK: Vermilion, 2008.

Furnham, A., *The Psychology of Behaviour at Work: The Individual in the Organisation*, UK: Psychology Press, 1997.

Goleman, D., *Emotional Intelligence: Why It Can Matter more than IQ*, UK: Bloomsbury Publishing, 1996.

Hanson, M.V and Allen, R.G., *The One-Minute Millionaire: The Enlightened Way to Wealth*, US: Three Rivers Press, 2002.

Harvard Business Review, *Harvard Business Review on Work and Life Balance*, US: HBS Press, 2000.

Hollands, J., *Red Ink Behaviors: Measure the Surprisingly High Cost of Problem Behaviors in Valuable Employees*, US: Blake Madsen Publishers, 1997.

Jennings, J., *Less Is More: How Great Companies Improve Productivity without Layoffs*, US, Porfolio, 2002.

Latham, G.P. and Yukl, Gary A. "A Review of Research on the Application of Goal Setting in Organizations", *Journal of Applied Psychology*, vol. 60, 1975, pp. 187–91.

Leimon, A. and McMahon, G., *Positive Psychology for Dummies*, UK: John Wiley & Sons, 2009.

Locke, E.A. and Latham, G.P., *A Theory of Goal Setting and Task Performance*, New Jersey: N.J. Prentice Hall Inc, 1990.

Luthans, F., *Organizational Behavior*, Singapore: McGraw-Hill, sixth edition, 1992.

McKenna, P., *Change Your Life in Seven Days*, UK: Bantam Press, 2010.

McKenna, P., *Instant Confidence*, UK: Bantam Press, 2006.

Maxwell, J.C., *The 21 Irrefutable Laws of Leadership*, US: Thomas Nelson Inc, 2007.

Moorhead, G. and Griffin, R., *Organizational Behavior*, US: Houghton Mifflin, 1995.

Montefiore, S. Sebag, *Speeches that Changed the World*, UK: Quercus Publishing Ltd, 2006.

Nicklaus, J., *Golf My Way: The Instructional Classic*, UK: Simon & Schuster, 2005.

Rinpoche, Yongey Mingyur and Swanson, Eric, *The Joy of Living: Unlocking the Secret and Science of Happiness*, UK: Bantam Books, 2007.

Robbins, A., *Notes from a Friend: A Quick and Simple Guide to Taking Charge of Your Life*, UK: Pocket Books, 2001.

Robinson, K. and Aronica, L., *The Element: How Finding Your Passion Changes Everything*, UK: Penguin, 2010.

Schlenger, S., and Roesch R., *How to be Organized In Spite of Yourself: Time and Space Management that Works with Your Personal Style*, US: New American Library, Penguin, 1999.

Seligman, Martin E.P., *Learned Optimism: How to Change Your Mind and Your Life*, US: Vintage Books, 2006.

Sharma, R., *The Greatness Guide*, UK: Harper Element, 2006.

Sharma, R., *Leadership Wisdom from the Monk Who Sold His Ferrari*, UK: Hay House Ltd, 2005.

Sharot, T., *The Optimism Bias: A Tour of the Irrationally Positive Brain*, US: Pantheon Books, 2011.

Tracy, B., *Eat that Frog! Get More of the Important Things Done – Today!* UK: Hodder and Stoughton, 2004.

Tolle, E., *A New Earth: Awakening to Your Life's Purpose*, UK: Penguin Books, 2005.

Tolle, E., *The Power of Now: A Guide to Spiritual Enlightenment*, UK: Hodder and Stoughton, 2001.

Vise, D.A., *The Google Story*, UK: Bantam Dell, 2005.

Walton, S., *Humanity: An Emotional History*, UK: Atlantic Books, 2004.

Warner, Bernhard, "Is Social Networking a Waste of Time?" www.thetimes.co.uk, 12 March 2008.

Wolff, J., *Focus: The Power of Targeted Thinking*, UK: Pearson Education, 2008.

Zander B. and Zander, R., *The Art of Possibility: Transforming Professional and Personal Life,* US: Penguin Books, 2002.

Zimbardo, P., and Boyd, J., *The Time Paradox: The New Psychology of Time that Will Change Your Life*, UK: Free Press, 2008.

index